First published in the United States of America in 2002 by
Rizzoli International Publications, Inc.
300 Park Avenue South
New York, NY 10010

© Flammarion, Paris, 2002
Numéro d'édition: FA0844
Dépot légal: juillet 2002

2003 2004 2005 2006 2007 / 10 9 8 7 6 5 4 3 2 1

Printed in Italy
on the presses of Grafedit, Bergame

ISBN: 0-8478-2514-0

Library of Congress Catalogue Control Number: 2002112219

Translation from the English and Adaptation of French Text: Hélène Bihery
Editorial Direction: Catherine Laulhère-Vigneau
Editorial Coordination: Cécile Degorce, Anne-Claire Meffre
Artistic Direction: Jean Guignebert
Proofreading: M. Poupard
Photoengraving: Sele Offset, Turin, Italy

Editor, English Edition: Christopher Steighner
Editorial Assistant, English Edition: Tiffany H. Sprague
Cover Design and Typesetting, English Edition: John Bernstein

**Preceding spread, left: Bayoubaisse (page 131).**

**Preceding spread, right: Jazz band in a New**

**Orleans street.**

70 CLASSIC RECIPES WITH A FRENCH ACCENT

# Cajun
# A Culinary Tour of Louisiana

## Judith Bluysen

PHOTOGRAPHS BY JEAN-MARIE DEL MORAL
FOOD STYLIST · ESIN DEL MORAL

RIZZOLI
NEW YORK

# Contents

# Louisiana

The swamps and plantations of Louisiana, as well as the city of New Orleans, are the birthplace of a regional American cuisine as complex, important and unique as the cuisines of Europe and Asia. Two distinctly different North American French populations formed the basis of this cuisine — the Cajuns and the Creoles.

Peasants and fishermen, the Cajuns sailed from their native regions of Poitou, Brittany, and Normandy along the western coast of France in the mid-seventeenth century to settle the French Canadian colony of Acadia, now Nova Scotia. Their refusal to swear allegiance to the British crown after the Treaty of Utrecht in 1713 resulted in the seizure of their property and their deportation to the English colonies of the Carolinas, New York, New England, and Maryland. Some repatriated to France, but they adapted badly and eventually found their way to the French colony of Louisiana in 1785. Others fled to the French Antilles, notably Santa Domingo, before immigrating to Louisiana in the mid-eighteenth century, settling in New Orleans and the surrounding southwestern regions known as the "French Triangle." Impoverished hunters, trappers, farmers, and fishermen, they adapted their ancestral recipes (which by now included some Acadian Micmac Indian savoir-faire) using the abundant fruits of the terrain and the bayous — the first hint of Cajun cuisine was born.

The term "Creole" is rather ambiguous, at first designating the descendants of the French aristocracy implanted in Louisiana, then encompassing as well Caribbean blacks, European transplants and their offspring, and the American-born descendants of African slaves. From 1769 through 1803

Preceding spread, clockwise from top left: Crawfish cabin in Breaux Bridge; Boiled crawfish; Garlic braids at the Farmer's Market in New Orleans; Interior of Mulate's restaurant in Breaux Bridge; Interior of Bruce's food factory in New Iberia; Bag of rice at Conrad Rice Cooperative in New Iberia; Bon Manger; Conrad Rice Cooperative.

Left: Oak Alley Plantation in Vacherie.
Above: Laura Plantation in Vacherie.

Above: In the Bayous, Atchafalaya River.
Below: Sign in New Orleans.
Right: Tea salon of Nottoway Plantation in White Castle.

Louisiana was under Spanish rule; by 1809 nearly 12,000 refugees — planters, slaves, and free blacks — had poured into Louisiana following the Santa Domingo revolution. They brought with them Caribbean spices, as well as the influences of classical French and Spanish cuisine. Wealthy and educated, they socialized with the descendants of the French aristocracy already installed around New Orleans, hosting frequent dinner parties, thereby fostering a cultural and culinary exchange. In 1803 Spain returned the region to France; twenty days later Napoleon sold the Louisiana Territory to the United States. The culinary result of all this turmoil was an abundance of kitchen personnel abandoned when their employers fled with the changing political winds and fortunes. Hired or acquired by the new nationality in power, the cooks adapted their repertoires; but a new spice, combination of ingredients, or technique inevitably found its way into the casserole and into the culture. Other nationalities or ethnicities also contributed to the culinary arts of southern Louisiana. A German colony was established in 1717, and although these settlers in fact preceded the Acadians, they became French-speaking and assimilated into the Cajun culture, bringing their expertise to *charcuterie*, *boucherie*, and beer brewing. There are African, Caribbean, and Native American Creoles, as well as people from Irish and Italian descent who, through marriage, birth, or just plain osmosis, have assimilated into the ever-evolving southern Louisiana civilization.

In culinary terms "Cajun" and "Creole" are often used interchangeably,

**Above: Chretien Point Plantation at sunset.
Right: Dancers at Mulate's restaurant in
Breaux Bridge.**

although there are differences in ingredients and in style. Historically, Louisiana Creole cooking is the cuisine of cooks and chefs. Although complicated in its European-based techniques, it is nevertheless subtle and delicate, often incorporating wines or liquors for the sauces. Cajun cooking, while as labor-intensive and flavor-rich, is a family project: a poor man's cuisine based on abundant indigenous ingredients hunted, raised, or gathered. (In southern Louisiana, oysters, crab, shrimp, and crawfish are plentiful, and everyone tends a garden.) Similar to Cajun cuisine is the African-Creole tradition now often called Soul Food, an African-American cuisine with some similarities in style and feeling to Cajun cooking but with different ingredients, spices, techniques, and of course history. It is essentially a family cuisine as well. A simple love of cooking, eating, and nourishing, and an appreciation of the social aspect of the table are what make these cuisines so special. These three separate but related styles of cooking are what define Louisiana cuisine today.

# About Spices

Cajun food has a reputation for being very spicy. Although it is true that this cuisine is generally more piquant than most of its European counterparts, when correctly prepared the spices serve to heighten the flavor of subtle combinations of vegetables, herbs, stocks, and fish or meat, never overwhelming them. Fresh herbs add a special zing when introduced after cooking, but crumbled or powdered dried herbs are often preferable in long-simmered gumbos and sauces as their flavors remain constant.

Cooking the spices matures the flavor and brings dimension to the dish. Careful timing of the addition of spices during the cooking period is necessary to achieve a proper balance. Some ingredients benefit from a "spice bath" before cooking (dry marinades or rubs), others harmonize with the spices during cooking, and many enjoy a subtle sprinkling of spices at the table.

"Blackening" is an untraditional cooking procedure invented by Paul Prudhomme, the Cajun chef who brought Louisiana cooking to the world's attention. The procedure for blackening is to coat both sides of the food (usually a firm fish or steak) with a spice mixture and to then sear it in a white-hot cast-iron skillet with little or no fat. This is another reason why powdered spices and herbs have their place in Cajun cuisine. In blackening, the burned spices form a crust that seals in the natural juices of the food, bestowing an incomparable texture and bite to the food, while permitting the inherent flavor to shine through. *This procedure creates a lot of spicy smoke — it is imperative to have a stove fan with a strong draw to pull out the smoke.*

### Typical Cajun Spices

Cayenne Pepper
Ground White Pepper
Ground Black Pepper
Paprika
Oregano
Ground Mustard
Garlic Powder
Onion Powder
Thyme

### Other Spices Used in our Recipes

Celery Salt
Coarse Sea Salt
Ground and Rubbed Sage
Cumin Seeds and Ground Cumin
Herbes de Provence
Rosemary
Mustard Seed

### Spice Mix for Cooking

This mixture is great to sprinkle on meat, chicken, or fish before cooking. It can also be used for blackening; in this case, add a bit of salt to the pan just before dropping in the meat or fish.

$\frac{1}{2}$ tablespoon ground Cayenne pepper
$\frac{1}{2}$ tablespoon ground white pepper
1 tablespoon paprika
1 tablespoon garlic powder
1 tablespoon onion powder
1 tablespoon herbes de Provence
1 tablespoon celery salt
2 tablespoons thyme
2 tablespoons oregano
2 tablespoons ground cumin

### Table Spice Mix

This mixture of spices and salt is perfect to sprinkle on cooked — especially fried — foods. Store it in a tightly closed container.

2 tablespoons paprika
2 tablespoons herbes de Provence
1 tablespoon garlic powder
1 tablespoon onion powder
1 tablespoon celery salt
1 teaspoon ground cayenne pepper
1 teaspoon ground white pepper
1 teaspoon coarsely ground black pepper
1 teaspoon ground cumin

# "First make a roux..."

is the usual beginning to a traditional Cajun recipe. The base for nearly all Cajun gumbos and sauces, a roux is a combination of flour and fat, stirred constantly over a medium flame until the desired shade of brown is achieved: peanut butter, chocolate, or nearly black. The roux serves two purposes: it imparts a smoky, nutty flavor to the sauce and it thickens it, giving it a velvety texture. The darker the roux, the more intense the flavor but the less thickening power. Most Cajun roux are chocolate-colored and use vegetable oil (sunflower, corn, or peanut), while French and New Orleans Creole recipes prefer paler, butter-based roux for more delicate and complicated sauces. Although vegetable oil is the traditional fat for Cajun roux, I've experimented with olive-oil based roux for some recipes and chicken fat for others, with delicious results.

The keys to successful roux making are organization — have all ingredients chopped, measured, and at hand — and patience. Plan on at least 20 minutes of nearly uninterrupted stirring for a dark roux. Lock the kids in a closet, put out the dog, and turn on the answering machine. Arm yourself with a wide, heavy-bottomed casserole (cast-iron cookware is perfect), and a long-handled whisk and spoon. Heat the oil until nearly smoking over a high flame and whisk in the flour, stirring constantly all over the bottom of the casserole. It will take nearly 5 minutes for the roux to color: first beige, next a face-powder hue, on to café au lait, milk chocolate, and finally, dark chocolate. If, at any point during the process, a black cloud appears on the roux, alas, there's nothing to do but toss it and start again: it has scorched and will taste bitter. These specks tend to appear at the café au lait stage so it's wise to pay particular attention at this point: lower the heat or remove the casserole from the flame from time to time and scrape the corners of the pot, where flour tends to stick. When the roux is the desired shade, turn off the heat and add all the vegetables at once, being very careful not to spatter yourself, as the roux is deceptively hot. The mixture will bubble frantically as the moisture from the vegetables evaporates; when it has calmed slightly, add the spice mixture. Next comes the hot liquid (hopefully, your homemade stock), which should be introduced gradually while stirring over a high flame, allowing the roux to come to a boil again before each addition. Then continue simmering as the recipe requires.

A word about materials: in Louisiana cuisine as well as classical French cuisine, some sauces and stews simmer for hours over low flames, which require heavy, good-quality cookware. Cast-iron pots and frying pans heat slowly and evenly and last a lifetime; with use and care they become naturally nonstick. Other practical items include a long-handled metal whisk for roux-making, metal tongs for easy handling of pieces of meat, and a long-handled slotted spoon to fish pieces of food from liquids.

# "First make a stock..."

is the first step for many of the recipes in this book. Honest homemade poultry, seafood, or vegetable bouillon is the basis for incomparable background flavor in gumbos, sauces, and rice dishes. Inexpensive, easy, and satisfying to make, stocks can be refrigerated up to five days or frozen indefinitely, in small, ready-to-use portions.

Once again, organize: If you want to make a chicken gumbo Saturday night, roast (or buy a roasted) chicken on Wednesday or Thursday and reserve the leftover bones and carcass to make a stock on Friday. Whenever you serve shrimp, let the heads and peelings boil while you clean up after dinner. Add a few onions and a turnip to leftovers from a cocktail crudités basket to make a vegetable stock the next day. The stock can be frozen if you won't be using it soon.

Canned stocks or bouillons can be somewhat successfully substituted in the recipes in this book; bouillon cubes slightly less so. But face it — nothing beats the real thing. Even if you are short on carcass weight or missing a vegetable, a homemade stock will always be superior. The proportions of all ingredients given in the following three recipes are variable; don't hesitate to use more carrots, for example, if you have carrots that need using. All stocks are intentionally undersalted and underseasoned; they are meant to be all-purpose.

**Above: Kitchen of the Laura
Plantation in Vacherie.**

# Chicken Stock

Cut all vegetables into ¼- to ½-inch pieces and brown them in a little vegetable oil in a large casserole over high heat. Add the chicken wings and carcasses — cooked or uncooked — and let them brown lightly. If you have a lot of uncooked pieces, first brown them in a 450°F oven for 20 to 30 minutes before adding them to the vegetables. Add the herbs and mix well. Pour in 5 quarts of cold water and bring to a boil. Skim the surface when foam appears. Once the stock boils, lower the heat and simmer for 2 hours. Strain in a large colander, pressing well to capture all the liquid. Let cool before refrigerating. Once cold, remove the fat that has risen to the surface.

# Fish Stock

Cut the vegetables in small pieces and lightly caramelize them in a small amount of vegetable oil. By coloring them you give a depth of flavor to the stock that will balance the strong flavor of the fish. Add the cleaned fish heads, bones, and shrimp shells, then the herbs and 5 quarts of cold water. Bring to a boil, skim, lower the temperature, and simmer for 1 hour. Strain the liquid and degrease if necessary.

# Shellfish Stock

The heads and shells of prawns, shrimp, crawfish, and langoustines, as well as the cooking water of any of the above, lend a remarkable flavor to this simplest of stocks. If you boil shrimp for Shrimp Remoulade or another dish where the shrimp are beheaded and peeled before serving, toss the heads and shells back into the pot and cook another 20 minutes. Or chop the heads off still-frozen shrimp and boil them in plain water with a few bay leaves (12 or so heads per 2 quarts of water, reduced to 1 quart after reduction) for a surprisingly shrimpy-flavored stock.

The strained leftover liquid from boiling or steaming crawfish, mussels, cockles, or any other shellfish also makes a wonderful base.

If you have fish heads, tails, and bones available, you can make a fish stock, which can be used alone or combined with a shrimp stock.

---

**CHICKEN STOCK**
**Yields approximately 3 quarts**

2 celery ribs with their leaves

2 onions with skin

1 whole leek, and any green parts left from another recipe

1 head of garlic, crushed

2 carrots any other odds and ends of vegetables lurking in the fridge, except peppers

5 pounds chicken wings, carcasses, or leftover chicken parts, except livers

4 bay leaves, 2 tablespoons or sprigs of thyme, and a bunch of parsley

---

**FISH STOCK**
**Yields approximately 3 quarts**

2 unpeeled onions and/or whole leeks

2 carrots

2 celery ribs with leaves

1 head of garlic, smashed

5 pounds fish bones and heads, well washed, and shrimp heads and shells

1 bunch of parsley, a few sprigs (or 2 tablespoons of dried) thyme, and 4 bay leaves

# Infusions

Herb infusions impart an unusual background flavor to sauces via stocks. They are made like tea using fresh or good-quality dried aromatic herbs — rosemary, thyme, sage, oregano, tarragon, bay leaves. Bring 1 quart of stock to a boil, toss in the herbs, turn off the heat, and let infuse 20 to 30 minutes. Strain. If you want a stronger flavor, reduce further. The resulting liquid can be used to deglaze cooking pans (as in Plantation Chicken, page 93) or when a little extra flavor is needed in a soup, sauce, rice dish, or stew.

# Vegetable Stock

An easy, inexpensive, all-purpose stock, this is extremely satisfying to make when you have odds and ends of vegetables threatening to decompose in your refrigerator. Use leek greens, celery and turnip leaves, mushroom feet, broccoli, spinach, herb and watercress stems, and any of these vegetables whole, plus onions and smashed garlic with their skins, carrots — nearly everything but peppers. Don't stint on your favorite fresh or dry herbs, plus a few bay leaves.

Pick over and wash all vegetables. They don't need to be beautiful, but cut off and discard all rotting or suspect parts. Chop everything in medium dice, mixing all together. Once cut, measure the approximate volume. Heat 4 tablespoons of olive oil in a large heavy-bottomed casserole and sauté the vegetables over medium-high heat, stirring frequently. Cover. Allow the vegetables to reach a deep golden color, without burning. Add herbes de Provence, some peppercorns, and 4 or 5 bay leaves. Cook a few minutes more. Add approximately 4 times the volume of water as the quantity of chopped, uncooked vegetables. Cover and bring to a boil; then remove cover and boil slowly for an hour or so until reduced by about one-third. Drain in a colander, pressing to remove every bit of liquid.

# Louisiana Classics

## Shrimp and Okra Gumbo

SERVES 6 TO 8

This gumbo is made without a roux, utilizing the okra juice as a thickener. Personally, I miss the smoky, nutty flavor and velvety texture of a Cajun roux, but it's a lighter gumbo and the pronounced flavor of the shrimp stock shines through on its own.

### THE STOCK

If the shrimp are frozen, defrost them. Remove the heads and shells, and make a shrimp stock as described on page 27, using 3 quarts of water to finish with 2 quarts of stock. Reserve the uncooked shrimp tails in the refrigerator.

### THE GUMBO

Cut 4 ounces (about one-fifth of the quantity) of the okra into ¼-inch rounds and reserve. (Discard the stem ends.) Mince the rest of okra, either by hand or in a food processor, and sauté them in the lard or vegetable oil with 1 teaspoon ground white pepper and ½ teaspoon cayenne pepper for 10 to 12 minutes. Add the onions and garlic and cook another 5 minutes, then add the tomatoes with their juice and 1 cup of shrimp stock and cook 15 minutes. Add the seasoning mix and the butter and cook an additional 5 minutes. Now add the remaining shrimp stock and bring to a boil. Lower the heat and simmer, uncovered, for 30 minutes. To serve, poach the shrimp in the simmering stock mixture, the reserved okra, and the scallion rounds 3 to 5 minutes, just until the shrimp are cooked. Serve immediately, with a large bowl of basmati rice.

**Seasoning Mix**

½ teaspoon ground white pepper
½ teaspoon ground cayenne pepper
½ teaspoon paprika
1 teaspoon salt
1 teaspoon thyme
1 teaspoon onion powder


4 to 6 shrimp or prawns per person, depending on size
1 pound fresh okra pods
3 tablespoons lard, duck fat, or vegetable oil
1 teaspoon ground white pepper
½ teaspoon ground cayenne pepper
1 large onion, finely chopped
4 garlic cloves, minced
1 sixteen-ounce can of crushed tomatoes, with juice
3½ tablespoons butter
2 quarts shrimp stock
2 whole scallions, or one white and light green part of a leek, finely chopped

**Above: Signs at Breaux Bridge.**

# Seafood Gumbo Calliope

SERVES 8

This dish was named in memory of our Chartreaux cat, Calliope; the gumbo's velvety texture and combination of delicate flavors is somehow very feline.

Heat the oil until it's very hot, and carefully add the flour, stirring constantly with a long-handled whisk. (See page 22 for more about roux-making.)

Once the roux is the color of dark chocolate, remove the pot from the heat and add all the vegetables at once. Be careful — the steam produced will be very hot! Continue stirring with the whisk until the bubbling calms a bit, then add the spices. Return the pot to the heat and slowly ladle in the hot stock. The gumbo should boil constantly during this process. After all the stock is incorporated, let the gumbo simmer for 30 minutes. At this point, you can continue with the recipe or let the gumbo sit for 1 to 2 hours on the stove, uncovered, while you do something else. To continue, just bring the gumbo back to a simmer.

**TO SERVE**

If you want to ascertain that everyone has the same amount and variety of seafood, divide the raw oysters, crawfish tails, and crabmeat equally among individual soup bowls, and pour a small amount of simmering gumbo just to cover the seafood. This process will poach the oysters and gently heat the crawfish and crabmeat. Slip the shelled shrimp into the pot of simmering gumbo and poach 2 minutes, just until the shrimp are cooked. Remove and place them in the soup bowls. Complete the individual bowls with gumbo, and either garnish with 2 tablespoons of cooked basmati rice, or pass a bowl of rice for each guest to help himself. Serve with a small dish of filé powder.

---

**Spice Mix**

$\frac{1}{2}$ teaspoon paprika

$\frac{1}{2}$ teaspoon ground cayenne pepper

$\frac{1}{2}$ teaspoon ground white pepper

$\frac{1}{2}$ teaspoon ground bay leaves, or 2 whole leaves

2 teaspoons salt

1 tablespoon ground oregano

1 tablespoon ground thyme

2 cups flour

2 cups vegetable oil

1 green bell pepper, diced

1 large onion, finely chopped

1 large celery rib, diced

3 garlic cloves, minced

3 quarts shellfish or fish stock, heated

24 shelled oysters (strain the liquor and add to the stock)

6 ounces crabmeat*

16 cooked crawfish tails

16 large shrimp or prawns, shelled

filé powder**

---

\* If you have access to live crabs, it will add to the flavor of the gumbo; if not, good-quality frozen or canned lump crab meat will do. If you use live crabs, cook them in the stock or use their cooking water as a base for your stock; if you buy whole, ready-cooked crabs such as Dungeness or stone, boil the shells in the bouillon you'll be using to make the gumbo after you remove the meat.

\*\* This spice, the ground leaves of the sassafras tree, is difficult to obtain outside of Louisiana. Aside from its subtle flavor, it is also used to thicken gumbos. Although traditional, it's not essential to this dish, but if you do use it, pass it at the table for each guest to add himself. It should never be cooked in the gumbo.

**Cajun dance hall in Lafayette.**

1 guinea hen (about 3 pounds), cut in 8 pieces
1 teaspoon each of salt, ground cayenne pepper,
and garlic powder

**Fry Dust**
1 ¼ cups flour
1 teaspoon salt
½ teaspoon ground cayenne
1 teaspoon garlic powder

vegetable oil for frying
3 Cajun andouille sausages or any good smoked
sausage, cut in ½-inch rounds
1 large onion, chopped
1 green bell pepper, finely chopped
2 celery ribs, finely chopped
2 garlic cloves, minced
3 quarts chicken stock
2 teaspoons thyme leaves
cooked basmati rice for garnish

# Guinea Hen Gumbo with Smoked Sausage

SERVES 6 TO 8

The Cajuns have interesting denominations of roux. A One-Beer Roux is a light roux that requires about 10 to 12 minutes of stirring, or the time it takes to drink a beer straight from the bottle; a Two-Beer Roux is a medium roux, 15 to 20 minutes or two beers; and a Three Beer Roux, the most flavorful with a luscious deep-chocolate color, takes 20 to 25 minutes of stirring

and drinking to achieve. Since I live in France now, I've tried this technique with wine, but since we nearly always use a dark roux...it can be hard to keep up!

Rub the hen with the mixture of 1 teaspoon each of salt, cayenne pepper, and garlic powder, and let sit at room temperature for a half hour. Mix fry dust ingredients, then place the hen pieces in a paper or plastic bag with the fry dust and shake to coat evenly. Remove the floured hen pieces and reserve 1 cup of the fry dust.

In a wide, heavy-bottomed casserole, heat 1 inch of oil and fry the hen pieces for approximately 12 minutes on each side. Drain on paper towels and allow to cool at room temperature. Brown the sausage rounds in this oil for about 3 minutes and reserve with the hen.

Carefully transfer the hot oil into another saucepan, wipe out the burned bits from the wide casserole, and pour back 1 cup of the hot oil, strained if necessary. Turn up the flame, and when the oil is very hot, add the reserved 1 cup of fry dust and begin whisking (see "First Make a Roux...," page 22). Whisk constantly until the roux is the color of milk chocolate. Remove the casserole from the heat and add all the veggies at once, stirring. They will produce a lot of steam, so keep your face away as you add them. When the steam subsides, return the pot to the heat and slowly add the hot stock, allowing the gumbo to return to the boil after each addition. Add the thyme, and let the gumbo simmer for 15 to 20 minutes, or until it has the consistency of heavy cream. While it's simmering, remove the meat from the bones, cut or tear into bite-sized pieces and add to the gumbo with the sausage. Adjust the seasoning; it's usually necessary to add more salt. Accompany with a bowl of basmati rice.

# Jambalaya

SERVES 6

The origin of the word jambalaya is widely speculated upon. Some claim it comes from the Spanish paella, both in name and in spirit; the French version favors "jambon à la ya" (*jambon*, French for ham; *ya*, an African word for rice). Probably the best-known Cajun specialty, jambalaya exists in as many versions as there are families who cook it, and it is served in all its variations in Louisiana homes of all races and origins. Essentially a poor man's meal, composed of leftover meats cooked with vegetables, rice, herbs, and spices, it has become a restaurant staple all over Louisiana, dressed up with shrimp or crawfish and served as an accompaniment or as a main course.

A colorful version of the origin of the name and the ascendance of jambalaya into restaurant fare involves a rural bayou restaurant in French-speaking Louisiana. The owner was just closing up after a busy Saturday night when a carload of unsavory characters charged into the oystershell parking lot and swarmed the restaurant demanding to be fed. Despite his protests that there was no food left, the unhappy boss was ordered to have the chef, Jean, rustle up some grub. In the privacy of the kitchen, he waved his hand at the remains of many meals and instructed the chef, "Jean, balai-la" ("Jean, sweep it all up").

In a wide, heavy pot, sauté the ham and sausage in 2 tablespoons of olive oil over high heat. Let the meat brown. It will stick to the bottom of the pan, but don't worry, just scrape. Add the spice mix and mix well with a wooden spatula, scraping and still not worrying about the mess stuck to the bottom of the pot.

**Cypress in the Bayous.**

Add the vegetables and garlic, stirring well. In about 3 minutes, when the bell pepper turns bright green, add the tomatoes with their juice. Mix once again, scraping the bottom of the pot. It's Cajun magic — the bottom of the pot is clean!) Once the mixture begins to boil, slowly add the rice. Allow to simmer 2 to 3 minutes before adding the stock and the 2 cups of tomato juice. When it begins to boil again, cover the pot and simmer on a very low heat for 20 minutes. The rice should steam and absorb all the liquid.

After the jambalaya is cooked, remove the casserole from the heat. Add the cooked shrimp and stir just to mix. Allow the jambalaya to sit uncovered in the pot for 5 minutes before serving. Garnish with whole cooked shrimp or crawfish.

**Spice Mix**

$1/2$ teaspoon ground cayenne pepper
$1/2$ teaspoon ground white pepper
$3/4$ teaspoon salt
$1/4$ teaspoon paprika
1 teaspoon herbes de Provence
$1/4$ teaspoon garlic powder
$1/4$ teaspoon onion powder

2 tablespoons olive oil
12 ounces smoked ham,
chopped into $1/2$-inch cubes
8 ounces Cajun andouille (or other smoked)
sausages, chopped into $1/4$-inch rounds
1 cup onion, chopped
1 cup celery, chopped
1 green bell pepper, chopped
4 cloves garlic, minced
1 large can (30 ounces) crushed tomatoes,
with juice
2 cups long-grain white rice
2 cups chicken or vegetable stock
2 cups tomato juice
$1/2$ pound small shrimp or crawfish,
cooked and shelled

# Duck Dirty Rice

## Spice Mix

½ tablespoon cayenne pepper
½ tablespoon celery salt
½ tablespoon ground white pepper
1 tablespoon ground cumin
1 tablespoon herbes de Provence
1 tablespoon oregano
1 tablespoon mustard seeds

7 ounces poultry gizzards, rinsed and dried
9 ounces *confit de canard* (preserved duck meat),
removed from the bone
½ cup onions, chopped
½ cup celery, chopped
½ cup green bell pepper, chopped
2 tablespoons garlic, minced
6 cups chicken or vegetable stock
2 cups basmati rice

### SERVES 8

In Louisiana, this recipe calls for fresh chicken livers and gizzards. In Paris, I've substituted *confit* duck gizzards and meat, which, when cooked until crispy, bestow a chewy texture and slightly smoky flavor to the rice. If you can't find the preserved gizzards and duck meat, substitute small bacon chunks for the gizzards and cubes of pastrami or smoked turkey for the duck. As in all rice dishes that are cooked covered, careful measuring of ingredients and careful timing are essential.

Chop the gizzards in small pieces. Cut the duck meat in ¼-inch cubes, with skin attached. In a large, heavy-bottomed pot, sauté the gizzards in 2 tablespoons of duck fat taken from the *confit* or vegetable oil (or lard), stirring frequently and scraping the bottom of the pot. This will take about 10 minutes; the gizzards will stick a bit to the bottom of the pot and become dark and dehydrated. Be careful not to get burned by spattered fat. When they are reddish brown and crispy, remove the gizzards from the pot and let them drain on paper towels.

In the same pot, leaving the residue from the gizzards, brown the duck meat over medium-high heat in 2 tablespoons of duck fat (or lard or vegetable oil) for about 5 minutes. Add the spice mix and cook 2 minutes, stirring and scraping; don't worry if the spices stick to the bottom of the pot. Add the vegetables, and voilà! — their moisture will clean the bottom of the pot. Stir and scrape often for 3 to 5 minutes, or until the bell peppers are a vibrant green. Add the stock and cook uncovered, over high heat, for exactly 10 minutes. The stock will begin to boil and reduce a little. Scrape the bottom of the pot to incorporate the last bit of caramelized spices into the liquid.

Slowly pour in the basmati rice, lower the heat to a minimum, and cover the pot. Cook 20 minutes. Remove the pot from the heat, and let the Dirty Rice rest 10 minutes, uncovered, stirring 2 or 3 times during that period. Add the reserved gizzards, stir, and serve.

# Red Beans and Rice

**SERVES 6 TO 8**

All over Louisiana, this dish was traditionally served for lunch on Mondays, which were washdays. It cooked all morning while the laundry was being done.

The night before, cover the beans with water — 2 inches above the beans — and soak. Drain just before cooking.

In a large, preferably cast-iron, casserole, brown the sausage pieces in the lard or olive oil, remove, and reserve. Place the ham hocks, vegetables, bay leaves and spice mix in the casserole with the fat from the sausages and 2 1/2 quarts of water. Cover and bring to a boil, lower the heat, and simmer, stirring occasionally, until the ham hocks are tender, about 1 hour. Remove the ham hocks and reserve with the sausages.

Drain the soaked beans and add them to the casserole with 1 quart of stock or water. Bring to a boil, lower the heat, and simmer for 30 minutes, stirring from time to time. Add 2 cups of water and continue cooking for 30 minutes, stirring often to prevent the beans from sticking to the bottom of the pot. Remove the meat from the ham hocks and add to the pot, along with the reserved sausage. Cook another 30 to 45 minutes, stirring regularly and scraping the bottom of the casserole, until the beans begin to burst. The sauce should be thick, but if it's dry, add a little water. Make sure that the beans don't stick to the bottom of the pot and burn. Add the Louisiana Hot Sauce or tabasco and cook another 10 minutes.

To serve, spoon a ring of cooked rice on a large platter, and mound the beans with the meats in the center.

**Spice Mix**
1 1/2 tablespoons herbs de Provence
1 teaspoon ground pepper
1 teaspoon ground cayenne pepper
1 teaspoon paprika
1 teaspoon ground cumin

2 cups dried red beans
1 pound Cajun andouille or any good smoked sausage, cut into 1/2-inch rounds
a little lard or olive oil
3 ham hocks
3 celery ribs, diced
1 green bell pepper, diced
1 large or 2 small onions, chopped
3 garlic cloves, smashed
5 bay leaves
1 tablespoon (or more to taste) Louisiana Hot Sauce or tabasco
basmati rice, cooked

# Blackened Fish

**SERVES 6 TO 8**

For this recipe, thick (nearly an inch) swordfish steaks or more delicate redfish fillets of a good half inch are best. You'll need a cast-iron frying pan and, above all, a good ventilation system as this technique produces lots of spicy smoke.

Mix all the spices and coat the fish well with them. Heat a cast-iron skillet over a high flame until white-hot, nearly 10 minutes. With the stove fan at maximum power, pour a little olive oil into the skillet and immediately drop in the fish. Cook 4 minutes, then carefully turn with a spatula. The spices will form a black crust and seal in the juices.

Cook 3 to 5 minutes (the redfish cooks more quickly than the swordfish) on the other side. Carefully remove the fish from the skillet and place on serving plates. Pour on a little melted butter and a squeeze of lemon before serving.

If your skillet is not large enough to accommodate all the fish at once, cooked pieces can be held in a 250°F oven, loosely covered with foil, while the others cook.

Blakened Fish is delicious with Roasted Rosemary Potatoes (page 132) and Pecan Green Beans (page 71).

**Spice Mix**
1/2 tablespoon cayenne pepper
1 tablespoon paprika
2 tablespoons ground cumin
1 tablespoon salt
1 tablespoon herbs de Provence
2 tablespoons oregano
1 tablespoon onion powder
1 teaspoon ground white pepper
2 teaspoons crushed thyme leaves
2 teaspoons garlic powder

# The Birth of a Restaurant

When my husband and I moved to Paris from New York City in 1986 we would never have foreseen a future in American cuisine. During his New York life, Frédéric sold French gourmet products to mostly French restaurants: foie gras, caviar, smoked salmon, etc.; I worked for a company that was the result of the first merger of a French and an American advertising agency. Many of our friends were French, we frequented French restaurants, drank French wines, and often cooked French cuisine at home. Frédéric was born in Paris and had spent his first twenty-four years there and in Cannes. He had brought me to France a few times on vacation. I'd adored it, happily scarfing down snails, stuffed goose necks, and wormy cheeses. Once ensconced there, I enthusiastically integrated myself and Frédéric happily reacclimated to Parisian life. Never did either of us yearn for tacos, hamburgers, or even bagels.

After a year, however, we were faced with moving back to New York or finding the means to stay in France. By this time I'd fallen irrevocably in love with crumbling stone, splintered beams, and other aspects of the country and its culture. But it was really the food that engaged me: hundreds of goat, cow, and sheep cheeses, runny, slick, or granular; abundant free-range poultry and game; an astonishing variety of fish and seafood available on nearly every city block. But I especially loved the vegetables: enormous heads of spiky frisée, tiny potatoes from the island of Noirmoutier, fat white asparagus, smoky artichokes, peppery arugula. And the things you could do with these ingredients! The idea of returning to New York and plastic-wrapped supermarket chicken parts was unbearable.

Interest in North American food had crept into France, perhaps as a result of affordable and accessible recreational travel, or the expansion of international corporations who shipped entire households abroad for a year or two stint at the overseas office. A few fledgling American restaurants and cookie emporiums sprang up. Jonathan Goldstein transformed his "Café Parisien" into "Coffee Parisian" and began serving "brunch all day, every day," as well as bona fide cheeseburgers and hot pastrami sandwiches. Avant-garde French chefs began experimenting with American recipes and *matières premières*. So when a former colleague of my husband, a restaurant supplier from Philadelphia, asked if we'd be interested in peddling American food products and ingredients in Paris, we jumped at the opportunity to remain in France.

We opened a boutique on Rue Pecquay, a tiny side street near the Pompidou Center. It took time for people to discover us but they did, and I was amazed not so much by the number of Americans missing, but by the increasing stream of French customers hunting the elusive peanut butter, spices and beans for chili, pancake mixes, and Napa Valley Cabernet Sauvignon.

The burgeoning interest in American cuisine intrigued me and I began work on a new project: an American takeout and catering activity. Through much trial and error, I learned it was possible to fabricate American regional specialties scratch using easily available ingredients. In fact, to no great surprise, I discovered the key ingredients for success in cooking are the quality of ingredients and the care in preparation.

In July 1990 we opened Thanksgiving, our restaurant on rue Beautreillis. The original idea was to sell American takeout, but as we already had the sources for grocery products from the United States, once again we installed shelves for packaged goods along the perimeter of the shop. A professional patisserie oven, an old stove with four burners, two stainless steel refrigerators, a freezer, and a cold case shared our thirty square meters of the Marais. By this time, the American community was larger and more organized: Disney, Microsoft, and IBM were flying over planeloads of personnel, and a couple of English-language publications provided perfect vehicles for advertising.

The first imperative to re-creating American cuisine "made in France" was finding the right basic ingredients. For me, it was essential to use fresh, local products rather than the frozen or otherwise processed specialty meats, sauce mixes, and pastry preparations that were beginning to appear on the scene concurrent with American and Tex-Mex fast-food and theme restaurants. Local butchers and greengrocers were fabulously patient and helpful by suggesting and often special-ordering for us strange cuts of meat, cases of green tomatoes, or baskets of African okra. We drew on an enormous bank of purveyors for such a tiny establishment, but we succeeded in acquiring just about everything we needed. The few items that we couldn't find in France, we imported or substituted with local ingredients.

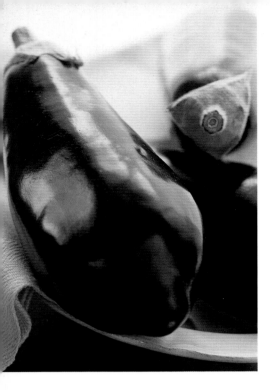

The reaction to our concept of regional American cuisine was immediate and encouraging. Our catering menu included specialties from various corners of the United States as well as original, regionally inspired buffet fare. We catered press presentations, sales meetings, business lunches, and book publications, as well as weddings and private parties. For Halloween, we carted backs tons of pumpkins from Paris's central wholesale market; during the Thanksgiving weekend we were overwhelmed with orders for roast stuffed turkeys, candied yams, and pecan and pumpkin pies. After three years the little red boutique on rue Beautreillis had become too small.

It was during a typical Parisian early morning September traffic jam, immobilized a few hundred meters from the boutique en route to deliver muffins and brownies to Galleries Lafayette, that we noticed a hand-lettered "For Rent" sign on the facade of a corner building. We called the phone number, examined the space, consulted an architect, negotiated for all of ten minutes, and signed the lease. Although needing some serious work, it contained a separate, good-sized space for a kitchen, a functioning bathroom, plus stone walls and oak beams that promised ambience. The first floor housed a pretty, high-ceilinged room, with one flat-surfaced stone wall inset with a raised column, and two windows overlooking the antique shops on rue St. Paul. Perfect office space, we fantasized. Our architect thought otherwise. "A restaurant," he urged. "It's the perfect space for a small restaurant."

Three whirlwind years of running an escalating catering business doesn't provide the skills and experience to successfully open and operate a restaurant. But like a *mauvaise herbe*, the idea had taken root and refused to die. Our friend Pascal, a chef who'd occasionally aided me on catering jobs, announced he was leaving the restaurant where he'd worked for years. A fugitive from Eurodisney restaurant management applied for a job — any job. Our window-washer's brother-in-law was looking for work as a dishwasher. It seemed as though the restaurant had decided to be. We sat up nights calculating fiscal improbabilities and chewing our nails, but finally acquiesced; we stretched our budget and purchased more kitchen equipment, ordered tables, chairs, and glasses, and investigated wines. A childhood friend, now a decorator working in Atlanta, Georgia, offered to scout around and send me the scavenged, beautiful mismatched china she uses to set her tables.

Brunch was a novelty in Paris when we opened the restaurant. We were among the first few restaurants to serve restorative drinks like Bloody Marys and Mimosas; Eggs Benedict; Blueberry Pancakes with strip bacon and maple syrup; and imported New York bagels with lox, cream cheese, and red onions. We are still the only restaurant serving the traditional Cajun sage-infused sausage called Boudin Blanc, topped with a dark roux-based brown beer sauce. Since brunch is such a part of our identity and our specialty, here are some recipes for some classic brunch dishes, many with a Cajun twist.

# Brunch Recipes
## COCKTAILS

## Café Nola

Serve in cognac glasses, topped with cinnamon sprinkled whipped cream.

_____

**For each glass:**

1 teapoon Kahlúa

1 teaspoon dark rum

1 teaspoon ameretto liqueur

1 demitasse cup of hot espresso

## Bloody Mary

Serve in tall glasses filled with ice, with a leaf-topped celery stalk as stirrer. Mix well.

_____

**For each glass:**

3 ounces vodka

¾ cup tomato juice

1 teaspoon Lea & Perrins Worcestershire sauce

1 teaspoon prepared horseradish

1 teaspoon fresh lime juice

1 pinch celery salt

1 small pinch ground white pepper

a few drops of Louisiana Hot Sauce

## Mimosa

Serve in champagne or white wine glasses.

_____

**For each glass:**

Juice of ½ orange, freshly squeezed

½ glass of champagne

## Plantation Punch

Serve in wine glasses or unusual glasses garnished with ice cubes in which you've frozen a maraschino cherry or other piece of fruit. Garnish each glass with an orange slice. This recipe yields 6 glasses.

_____

**Mix in a pitcher:**

6 ounces white rum

3 ounces dark rum

1¼ cups fresh grapefruit juice

1¼ cups fresh orange juice

3 ounces grenadine syrup

**Left: Bloody Mary. Right: Mimosa.**
**Following spread, left: Plantation Punch.**
**Following spread, right: Café Nola.**

# Eggs Benedict

Melt the butter and allow to return to room temperature. In a small, heavy-bottomed saucepan, mix the egg yolks, water, and vinegar. Vigorously beat this mixture with a whisk either over a larger pan of simmering water (bain marie) or directly over a low flame or burner, removing the pan from time to time as you whisk to avoid cooking the mixture too quickly. When the foam subsides and the mixture is very thick and creamy and the whisk begins to leave furrows on the bottom of the pan, immediately remove the pan from the heat and slowly incorporate the butter while whisking. Beat just until the sauce is homogenously thick, with a surface sheen. Season with salt and pepper and set aside. Never attempt to reheat this sauce —

it will collapse. As you ladle the sauce over the hot poached eggs, the residual heat from the eggs will sufficiently warm the sauce.

Cut the English muffins in half and toast them while you lightly fry the Canadian bacon. On each serving plate, top each half of an English muffin with a slice of the fried bacon.

Poach the eggs 2 to 3 minutes in lightly vinegared simmering water. Place each poached egg on a bacon-covered half of an English muffin and drizzle with the hollandaise sauce. Serve immediately.

## VARIATIONS

The bacon can be replaced by smoked salmon (Eggs Irish) or by creamed spinach (Eggs Florentine).

**For each serving:**

1 English muffin
2 slices of Canadian bacon
2 poached eggs
Hollandaise Sauce

**Hollandaise Sauce**

For a successful emulsion, it's paramount that the melted butter return to room temperature.
1 cup (2 sticks) melted butter
4 egg yolks
2 tablespoons water
1 teaspoon white vinegar
a pinch of salt and pepper to taste

# Pecan Pancakes

YIELDS APPROXIMATELY 10 PANCAKES

Mix the dry ingredients in a small bowl. In a large bowl, beat the egg and whisk in the milk. With a large spoon, mix the dry ingredients into the liquid just until the flour is moistened; small lumps are a good sign. Incorporate the melted butter without over-mixing. The batter should resemble oatmeal. Gently fold in the pecan pieces.

Heat a cast-iron skillet or a heavy nonstick pan until a sprinkled drop of water sizzles and evaporates. With a kitchen towel, rub the pan with a tiny bit of lard or bacon fat. Using a small ladle or a large spoon, pour

about ¼ cup of batter into the hot skillet with a circular motion. In a minute or two, the edges will begin to set and tiny bubbles will appear and burst in the pancake. When this occurs, turn the pancake and cook another 2 minutes. Serve immediately with butter and maple syrup, accompanied by grilled bacon slices.

## VARIATIONS

For blueberry pancakes, add 1 tablespoon of fresh or still-frozen blueberries per pancake to the batter just before cooking; for chocolate chip pancakes, 1 tablespoon of chips, and serve with whipped cream instead of syrup.

1 ¾ cups flour
3 tablespoons sugar
2 ½ teaspoons baking powder
1 teaspoon salt
1 egg
1 cup whole milk
3 tablespoons melted butter
¾ cup pecans, coarsely chopped
Lard or bacon fat to grease the pan

# Eggs Sardou

Preheat the oven to 450°F. Place the artichoke bottoms on an ovenproof pan and fill with about 2 tablespoons of the Crab Stuffing. Drizzle a little olive oil over the stuffing and bake for 6 to 10 minutes, just until the crab is lightly browned. Remove

from the oven and place on serving plates. Poach the eggs 2 to 3 minutes in lightly vinegared simmering water, then place them on the crab stuffing and drizzle on the hollandaise sauce. Serve immediately.

**For each serving:**

This version of Eggs Sardou, a popular New Orleans brunch item, is a tasty way to use up any leftover Crab Stuffing (page 86).
2 cooked artichoke bottoms
4 tablespoons Crab Stuffing (page 86)
2 eggs
Hollandaise sauce (see above, and use Pernod or Herbesaint instead of the vinegar)

## Muffins

YIELDS 12 MUFFINS

To the basic muffin recipe given here, you can add fresh or frozen berries (if using frozen, add the still-frozen fruit to the batter just before baking); chocolate chips, or candied fruits. The carrot cake recipe (page 143) also makes yummy muffins.

Preheat the oven to 375°F. Mix the first 4 ingredients and reserve. In a large bowl, beat the eggs with the sugar. Add the milk, vanilla, and the butter. Beat with a whisk until the batter is homogenous. Pour the flour mixture into the batter and stir with a spoon or spatula just until moistened — don't overmix. A few small lumps are the desirable sign of a light hand. Add the fruit or chocolate chips, if desired. Spoon the batter into the paper-lined or greased muffin pan three-quarters full and cook 15 to 20 minutes, until the tips are split and browned. Allow to cool 10 minutes before removing from the pans.

2 cups flour
1 tablespoon baking powder
$\frac{1}{2}$ teaspoon salt
$\frac{1}{4}$ teaspoon nutmeg (optional)

2 eggs
$\frac{3}{4}$ cup sugar
1 cup whole milk
2 teaspoons vanilla extract
5 ounces melted butter

## Pumpkin Muffins

YIELDS 18 MUFFINS

Preheat the oven to 375°F. Mix the dry ingredients in a small bowl and set them aside. Beat the oil and the sugar together with a whisk or in a mixer. Add the pumpkin, the vanilla, and the eggs, one by one, while mixing. Add the dry ingredients and mix just until moistened. Fold in the pine nuts, if desired. Fill a paper-lined or greased muffin pan three-quarters full and bake 25 minutes. Allow to cool in the pan 10 before removing the muffins.

3 cups flour
1 $\frac{1}{2}$ tablespoons baking powder
$\frac{1}{2}$ teaspoon salt
1 teaspoon ground cinnamon
1 teaspoon ground ginger
$\frac{1}{2}$ teaspoon allspice

$\frac{3}{4}$ cup vegetable oil
2 cups sugar
1 can (15 ounces) solid packed pumpkin
2 teapoons vanilla extract
3 eggs

$\frac{1}{2}$ cup pine nuts, toasted (optional)

# Thanksgiving

In November, our Parisian restaurant, catering service, and grocery store — all of which are aptly named Thanksgiving — loom large. The concept of the Thanksgiving holiday is still quite exotic for most French people, and we go to great lengths to introduce the joys of the Thanksgiving table to Parisians. As a native New Yorker, I just can't bypass the traditional Thanksgiving menu of my childhood, but I have added a few Cajun accents, such as pecans in the cornbread stuffing and in the green beans. In Louisiana, the Creoles celebrate this holiday in much the same way as we Yankees, but with the addition of several "dressings" — oyster, rice, crawfish — served as accompaniments to the turkey. The Cajuns, who didn't really consider themselves American until not long ago, don't have a Thanksgiving tradition. But, in recent years the Cajuns have developed a few intriguing Thanksgiving recipes, such as deep-fried turkey and turduckey (turkey stuffed with a whole duck, which is often itself stuffed with a quail). Need I mention the quantity of turkey gumbo served statewide in early December?

But wherever you live, Thanksgiving is a holiday that brings the whole nation together around the table, and the origins of this truly American holiday are often forgotten after our school days. It's worth repeating here, as it embodies in its melding of Native American and European cultures a correlative of the same sort of culinary exchange that occurred among the early Louisianians.

**Preceding spread: Oak tree near White Castle.**
**Left: Dining room at Nottoway Plantation.**
**Above: Room at Mulate's restaurant.**

The story begins with Squanto and Samoset, two Native Americans from different east coast Algonkian-speaking tribes. They first met each other in England, where they had both journeyed with English explorers in the early seventeenth century. In 1620 they returned to the new world together, to Squanto's home, a northern coastal village named Patuxet. But the village had been wiped out by smallpox carried by European explorers, so they camped with a neighboring Wampanoag tribe. The following spring, hunting by the beach near Patuxet, they came across a group of sickly, starving English pioneers. After warily observing them for a few days, Squanto and Samoset decided to approach the strangers, greeting them in the English they had learned abroad. The Native Americans' ability to communicate in English disarmed the immigrants, who gratefully accepted Squanto's offer to teach them to cultivate the inhospitable land. Over the spring and summer months the settlers learned to grow and harvest corn, dig clams, tap maple trees for syrup, use fish for fertilizer, make medicine from plants, preserve meat, and build suitable housing for the winter months ahead. Autumn arrived; the Pilgrims were in better shape than they'd been since leaving England. In observation of their own religious harvest rituals, in addition to an uncharacteristic benevolence of spirit, they decided to celebrate their survival. Miles Standish, leader of the Pilgrims, invited Squanto, Samoset, Chief Massasoit of the Wampanoags, and their immediate families to a three-day feast.

He had greatly underestimated the size of the families, however, and there was not enough food for the ninety or so Native Americans who arrived. Harvest festivities were nothing new to the Wampanoags, who celebrated six per year, so Chief Massasoit sent a delegation home for more food. And so it was that the First Thanksgiving included wild turkey, venison, squash, cornbread, and cranberries. Native American men and women dined together seated at a table instead of habitual fur throws on the ground; the Puritan women remained standing behind their husbands until the men had finished, as was their custom. A peace and friendship agreement was reached between Standish and Massasoit, and the Pilgrims were given the former Patuxet clearing on which to construct their village of Plymouth.

The first official Thanksgiving of the embryonic United States of America was celebrated by General George Washington and his army in 1777, in an open field en route to Valley Forge, Pennsylvania. President Washington's first proclamation after his election as the first president of the nation, in 1789, declared November 26, 1789 as a national day of "thanksgiving and prayer." Yearly presidential thanksgiving proclamations continued until the early 1800s, then ceased for forty-five years until President Abraham Lincoln resumed them in 1863. In November 1941 President Franklin Delano Roosevelt signed a bill establishing the fourth Thursday in November as Thanksgiving Day.

In November 1995, my restaurant staff and I set about planning the first Thanksgiving in Paris, which, for reasons having nothing to do with historical

**Right: Cranberry Sauce (page 68).**

accuracy, would be a three-day feast: Thursday evening, plus Friday and Saturday lunch and dinner. Even with a couple of borrowed tables and chairs, restaurant capacity was strained at twenty-four; but as Thanksgiving Thursday isn't a French holiday, we could accommodate people unable to celebrate during the week by continuing the feast throughout the weekend. Finding quality fresh turkeys in November was no longer a problem. Friends in rural southwest France had introduced us to a turkey farmer who raised, especially for our holiday, *dindes fermières* so tender, juicy, and flavorful that orders nearly doubled every year. From the boutique, we sold them ready to cook or cooked and stuffed to order. During the Thanksgiving weekend, our local butcher rented us one of his *rôtissoires*, as well as his son-in-law to run it. From Rungis, the central wholesale market located just outside of Paris, we carted back truckloads of the world's biggest and best yams, imported from Israel, as well as cartons of fresh American cranberries. Our entire extended staff worked seemingly round-the-clock baking pecan, pumpkin, and apple pies, plus cheesecakes, cornbread for stuffing, casseroles of candied yams, and gravy for the birds; organizing catering and pick-up orders; and ringing up record grocery sales in the boutique. Over fifty gallons of homemade cranberry sauce jelled in our walk-in refrigerator side-by-side with uncountable numbers of pumpkin pies. When the restaurant was fully booked for Thursday, Friday, and Saturday evenings, takeout orders multiplied out of control. The Wednesday before Thanksgiving Day, inspectors from France Telecom arrived to investigate overloaded neighborhood circuits. We took the phones off the hook and concentrated on filling existing orders, cooking, and restocking shelves. It's satisfying to play the role of cultural ambassador, especially when it means bringing so many dislocated Americans, of all ethnic origins, with native Parisians to enjoy this most American of holidays.

**Left: Kitchen at the Laura Plantation.**
**Above: Carriage from Acadian Village in Lafayette.**

# Roast Turkey

In the United States, despite the recent trend toward free-range fowl, enormous frozen turkeys, often injected with an additive that purports to keep the bird moist during the cooking period, are the norm. One of the joys of preparing a Thanksgiving meal in France is the quality of turkey available; free-range turkeys are the best, but even a fresh, good-quality regular turkey correctly roasted is delicious. In Paris we tend to use smaller birds, 13 pounds or less, as we have smaller ovens and live in apartments, and Thanksgiving is not yet the whole-extended-family tradition that it is in America. The following recipes are based on a 13-pound turkey, enough for twelve adults, which in fact is better suited to today's smaller family sizes in America and France.

You will need a heavy roasting pan, large enough to accommodate the turkey with room at the bottom to access the basting juices. A bulb baster is a great tool and prevents wrist burns.

Plan on 1 pound of ready-to-cook turkey (weight after head, feet, and innards are removed) for each person to be served. Generally the smallest turkey weighs about 7 pounds. Preheat your oven very hot (450°F). Rub the outside of the bird with butter or goose fat, and season the cavity with salt, pepper, and herbes de Provence. Stuff just before putting in the oven, about three-quarters full to allow the stuffing to expand during cooking. Roast at this high temperature 10 minutes, then lower the heat to 350°F. Plan on 18 minutes of cooking time per pound for a stuffed bird under 4 1/2 pounds; for larger or unstuffed turkeys allow 30 to 35 minutes. If you have a convection oven, roasting time should be cut by about 20 percent. Baste with the rendered juices every 20 minutes or so, squirting a bit of juice into the cavity from time to time to keep the exposed stuffing moist. If the top of the turkey is close (1 1/2 inches or less) to the roof of the oven, tent loosely with foil after the turkey has browned to prevent burning. Large turkeys also benefit from a loose foil covering after browning.

About 20 minutes before the end of planned cooking time, prick the part of the thigh closest to the body with a knife. If the juices run clear or yellow, the turkey is done. If the juices are pink, return the turkey to the oven and try again in 10 minutes. After the turkey is cooked, allow it to stand at room temperature for 20 minutes before removing the stuffing and carving the bird.

## THE GRAVY

YIELDS APPROXIMATELY 4 CUPS

Our gravy is the degreased turkey cooking juices thickened with a medium roux. It can be started in advance with a rich poultry stock, and the turkey cooking juices added just before serving.

Melt the butter in a heavy-bottomed saucepan. Add the flour and whisk constantly over a low heat. When the roux is the color of toast, raise the heat and slowly incorporate the stock, continuously stirring. Be careful; it will be very hot.

Bring to a boil, lower the heat, and simmer 15 to 20 minutes. If not serving right away, set it aside. When the turkey is cooked, degrease its cooking juices and add them to the gravy while reheating. If it's too thick, add a bit more stock; if too thin, simmer a few minutes to reduce it.

---

4 tablespoons butter (or pure poultry fat)
4 tablespoons flour
1 quart rich poultry stock plus the turkey cooking juices (about 3/4 cup)
salt and ground white pepper to taste

## HERBED CORN BREAD STUFFING

A good stuffing is everybody's favorite component of the Thanksgiving meal, and there is never enough. The following recipe is basic; you can add mushrooms, bacon, water chestnuts, apples, cooked chopped liver, etc. Enough for a 13-pound turkey, this recipe can be doubled and the extra stuffing can be cooked on top of the stove and mixed with the stuffing cooked in the bird.

---

1 quart of mixed stale (hard) breads,
at least 1/2 corn bread (page 149), broken into very small pieces to crumbs
1 onion, finely chopped
2 to 3 celery ribs, finely chopped
1/2 cup pecan pieces, or walnuts, coarsely chopped
2 tablespoons herbes de Provence
1 tablespoon sage leaves, crumbled
1 teaspoon celery salt
1 teaspoon freshly ground pepper

Mix everything together and reserve in the refrigerator overnight in a tightly closed container or plastic bag, so the humidity from the vegetables can permeate the bread. Just before putting the turkey in the oven, fill the cavity 3/4 full.

To cook the stuffing on the stove, use the same ingredients as above. Melt 1/2 cup of butter in a large pot. Add the bread, spices, and vegetables and mix with a wooden spoon until all of the butter is absorbed and well distributed, about 5 minutes. Raise the heat, make a well in the center of the stuffing, and slowly add 1 cup of chicken stock. Stir thoroughly; when steam begins to rise, lower the heat to a minimum, cover the pot, and allow to steam for 10 minutes, stirring once or twice to prevent burning. When the stuffing is hot, remove the pot from the heat and set aside, covered, for 15 minutes. This stuffing should be moist but not saturated — if it's too wet, allow to stand uncovered or return it to the heat and cook uncovered for a few minutes, stirring constantly. If it's too dry, add a little stock. Serve as is or mix it with the stuffing cooked in the bird.

# Candied Yams

SERVES 12

**This recipe can be prepared the night before and baked while the turkey is cooling.**

Preheat the oven to 400°F and bake the sweet potatoes in their skins about 1 hour, until a fork can easily pierce them. Allow to cool, and the skin will zip right off. Once peeled, cut into rounds of about ¹/₂ inch. In a buttered baking dish, make three layers of yams, sprinkling each with brown sugar, nutmeg, cinnamon, and butter. The top layer should be well covered with sugar, butter, and spices. Cover and refrigerate if you've prepared them in advance. One half hour before serving, bake the uncovered casserole 20 minutes in a preheated 400°F oven.

---

6 pounds fresh orange sweet potatoes or yams
(or 5 to 6 cans)
1 cup dark brown sugar
1 tablespoon ground nutmeg
2 tablespoons ground cinnamon
1 cup butter, cut in small pieces

# Cranberry Sauce

YIELDS APPROXIMATELY 2 CUPS

---

1 twelve-ounce bag fresh cranberries
1 cup granulated sugar
¹/₂ cup water
¹/₂ cup Cointreau
zest of 12 oranges

**Cranberries are indigenous to North America, and are cultivated mostly in the cold bogs of New England, New Jersey, and the Great Lakes. They are in the same family as the European and Scandinavian lingonberries, but cranberries are larger and harder. This classic recipe makes a relish that can be served cold or at room temperature as a condiment to the turkey.**

Rinse the cranberries, discarding any that are soft or rotten. Boil the sugar, water, Cointreau, and orange zest. Add the cranberries, lower the heat and simmer just until the berries burst, about 10 minutes. Allow to come to room temperature and then refrigerate to jell the sauce. This keeps a good 2 weeks in the refrigerator, so make it in advance.

# Pecan Green Beans

SERVES 12

Remove the ends of the green beans. In a large pot, bring unsalted water to a boil and toss in the green beans. Cook just until the water returns to a boil, then drain and plunge the beans into cold water to stop the cooking and set the bright green color.

Reserve. Just before serving, melt the butter in a pan large enough to accommodate all the beans and briefly sauté the pecans. When the butter foams, add the green beans and mix well to coat. Sprinkle with the coarse salt and crushed black pepper, and serve.

1 1/2 pounds very thin fresh green beans
5 tablespoons unsalted butter
2 cups pecans, coarsely chopped
sel de Guérande, or coarse sea salt, and crushed black pepper

# Glazed Ham

SERVES 8 TO 12

**This ham is traditionally served at Thanksgiving, Christmas and Easter, but is also enjoyed at other family get-togethers. As good cold as it is hot, it's terrific picnic or outdoor fare. With Cole Slaw (page 110), Cajun Potato Salad (page 115), and Buttermilk Biscuits (page 149), it's perfect for the Fourth of July.**

Preheat the oven to 350°F. Place the ham in a baking dish, fatty-side up. With a small, sharp knife, cut parallel lines 3/4 inch apart, but not too deep, beginning from the top left of the ham and finishing at the bottom right. Then start again at the top right of the ham and draw the lines to the bottom left. Stick a clove in each intersection. (If you're over forty, get out your reading glasses.) Cook the ham for about 1 to 1 1/2 hours, depending on the size. It should be lightly golden at this point.

While the ham cooks, prepare the glaze: mix the brown sugar in the honey, crushing any lumps with a wooden spoon. Add the mustard, spices, and the hot sauce and mix until smooth. While it should be thick, it should mix easily. If it doesn't, add a bit more honey.

After the ham has cooked, remove from the oven and coat with the glaze, using the back of a large spoon. The heat from the ham will spread the glaze, little pressure is necessary. Be careful not to pull out the cloves while spreading the glaze. Put the ham back into the oven and bake 30 minutes, or until the glaze is medium brown and uniform.

Allow to cool 20 minutes before carving.

Note: If your oven cooks unevenly, turn the ham around once or twice during the cooking process, to ensure even color.

1 six- to twelve-pound ham, on the bone, lightly smoked
whole cloves
2 cups dark brown sugar
1/2 cup honey
4 tablespoons Dijon mustard
2 teaspoons cinnamon
2 teaspoons ground ginger
1 teaspoon ground nutmeg
1/2 teaspooon allspice
1 tablespoon Louisiana Hot Sauce or tabasco

# Smashed Potatoes

3 pounds Idaho potatoes

4 garlic cloves, smashed and peeled

1 large onion, peeled and quartered

2 tablespoons coarse salt

2 bay leaves

5 tablespoons unsalted butter,
cut in small pieces

1 cup crème fraîche or heavy cream

½ tablespoon ground sage or nutmeg

salt and pepper to taste

SERVES 6 TO 8

**In this recipe, we boil the potatoes in their skins with onion and garlic, and mash them roughly by hand before incorporating cream and butter.**

Scrub and rinse the potatoes well but do not peel. Cut in 1-inch pieces. Place the cut potatoes, garlic, onion, coarse salt, and bay leaves in a large pot and cover with cold water. Bring to a boil and cook 20 minutes, or until a piece of potato falls from an inquiring knife. Drain in a colander. Remove bay leaves.

Return the potatoes and vegetables to the dry cooking pot. Smash with a potato masher or a large fork. Little by little, incorporate the butter and cream, mixing with a large spoon. Add the sage and 1 teaspoon each of salt and pepper. Taste and adjust the seasonings if necessary. Serve immediately or reheat, covered, in a microwave.

# Pecan Pie

2 cups pecans, chopped
(reserve 8 halves for decoration, if desired)

3 tablespoons dark rum

1 recipe Pâte Sucrée (page 139)

½ cup light brown granulated sugar

1 tablespoon flour

2 tablespoons unsalted butter, melted

½ tablespoon vanilla extract

½ teaspoon salt

3 beaten eggs

½ twelve-ounce bottle dark Karo syrup

SERVES 8

Soak the pecans in the rum. Set aside. Roll out the dough and line an ungreased 9-inch pie pan with it. Place in the refrigerator while you make the filling. Preheat the oven to 350°F.

In a large bowl or a mixer, beat the sugar, flour, butter, vanilla, and salt. Add the eggs; once the mixture is homogenous add the Karo syrup. Stir in the rum-soaked pecans and pour the mixture into the pie pan. Decorate with the reserved pecan halves.

Place the pie on the preheated baking sheet and bake 45 to 50 minutes. Allow to cool before cutting.

1 recipe Pâte Brisée (page 139)

1 cup sugar

1 teaspoon cinnamon

1 teaspoon ground ginger

½ teaspoon ground nutmeg

¼ teaspoon ground cloves

½ teaspoon salt

2 whole eggs plus one yolk (reserve the white to
waterproof the inside of the crust)

1 fifteen-ounce can of pumpkin

1 ½ cups heavy cream

# Pumpkin Pie

### SERVES 8

Roll out the dough and fit it into a 9-inch pie pan. Paint the inside with the reserved egg white. Preheat the oven to 425°F.

Mix the sugar, spices, and salt in a small bowl. In a large bowl, beat the eggs and whisk in the pumpkin and the sugar mixture. Once smooth, slowly incorporate the cream. Pour into the pie pan. Bake in the lower part of the oven for 15 minutes, then turn the oven down to 350°F and continue to bake 40 to 45 minutes, until a knife inserted in the center comes out clean. Allow to cool 2 hours before serving.

**Right: Cajun interior at Acadian
Village in Lafayette.**

# New Orleans

More than 150 years before Auguste Escoffier wrote *Le Guide Culinaire* (1903), which organized the many French regional cuisines into what is now known as traditional or classical French cuisine, Madame Langlois, housekeeper to New Orleans's Governor Bienville, was giving cooking classes to the women of the settlement. In 1722, during the early days of French colonization, a flock of fifty or so disgruntled housewives marched on the governor's mansion, banging pots and pans, to protest the paucity of spices and other imported luxuries available to them and their cooks in the New World. This became known as the Petticoat Rebellion, and Madame Langlois was able to enliven the standard household fare of rice and cornmeal mush by passing on her culinary expertise garnered from the Choktaw tribe of Native Americans. She taught the women how to use ground sassafras leaves to thicken and add taste to gumbos, and how to prepare the many local river fish and game. This was the precursor of Creole cuisine, amplified and refined over the years by the European cooks who immigrated to the New Orleans settlement. In fact, more than any other regional American fare, Creole cuisine is continually changing, due to the ongoing influences of European gastronomy.

Creole cuisine came to have a great influence over our restaurant in Paris by a fortuitous reversal of the Europe-to-New Orleans immigration flow. The first waitress at our restaurant in Paris was a very talkative New Orleans native named Susan who often reminisced about Louisiana lifestyle and

**Preceding spread, left: Live crawfish.**
**Preceding spread, right: Bar in New Orleans.**
**Left: Building in the French Quarter in New Orleans.**
**Above: Sign for a bar in New Orleans.**

Above: Shrimp cabin at Breaux Bridge.
Right: Café near the Farmer's Market in New Orleans.

cuisine. Although we'd been dishing up jambalaya since our opening on rue Beautreillis and included a duck and oyster gumbo on our regional menu, it was Susan's wry renditions of the Louisiana relationship to food that finally focused our attention on the state and its cuisine: she told stories of the telescoping forks her family uses to spear tidbits off each other's plates and how it's essential to order your po' boys "drippin' te th' elbows" if you don't want to be marked as a tourist at Mother's. Our interest piqued, we bought, borrowed, and stole Louisiana cookbooks and spent our precious days off cooking Louisiana classics. Our daily specials were more often than not of Louisiana origin. Vacations found us in New Orleans, Lafayette, and Baton Rouge, eating three meals per day in various food establishments — gourmet and family restaurants, open-air festivals, and in people's homes whenever we could cadge invitations. We soon realized that obsession with good food, good cooking, and good eating is endemic to that region and that this French-accented piece of America certainly merited further attention.

New Orleans, like Paris, is historically a city about food and drink. For the traveler or tourist, it is about restaurants — in the *Vieux Carre*, the French Quarter, they are lined up one after the other: old, new, fancy, casual, and gourmet. The venerable dining institutions — Galatoire's, Antoine's, Arnaud, and Broussard — comprise the "old guard" restaurants; Paul Prudhomme's K-Paul's, Emeril Lagasse's Nola and Emeril's, and the Brennan family's various

This page, top: Delivery truck.
This page, above: Sign for the
Louisiana police.
Right: Seafood restaurant in
New Orleans.
Page 85: Sign for the Farmer's
Market in Louisiana.

enterprises represent the newer, "star chef" progeny. Take-away stands sell daiquiri and other alcoholic fruit juice–based concoctions in huge paper cups with lids and straws, called "Go-Cups"; you can buy beer like that, too, as it is illegal to drink from glass on the streets of New Orleans. The sandwich shops offer intriguing compilations — the Central Grocery across the street from the French Market is famous for their *muffalatas* — two-inch thick, round monsters crammed with slices of proscuitto, mortadella, provolone, and a fabulous secret dressing of marinated chopped olives, grilled peppers, onions, cauliflower, and garlic. Voluptuous po' boys, piled with roast beef, lettuce, tomatoes, mayonnaise, mustard, pickles, and slivers of onions; or fried oysters, tartar sauce, and various condiments give a different definition to the word "sandwich."

Louisiana culture seems to revolve around food, and the fabled Southern hospitality manifested itself at Susan's family's home, where her parents initiated us to the joys of authentic Louisiana cuisine, the kind you know if you're native. Shrimp Remoulade, a summer Seafood Gumbo made with shrimp and lump crabmeat, Dirty Rice cooked with fresh chicken livers, a Green Bean Étouffée with smoked tasso ham, and various tastes and tidbits of family cuisine were served up with a generous amount of information, anecdotes, and lore. We made a date with them for the following Sunday at Galatoire's, one of New Orleans's legendary Creole dining institutions dating from the turn of the century.

Most New Orleans natives have their preferred old-guard restaurant where they dine automatically; usually, it's an inherited preference. They also have their preferred waiter; often as not, he's also been the favorite waiter, or descendant of the favorite waiter, of the family for generations. Galatoire's was Susan's family's *cantine*. As the restaurant didn't then take reservations, we stood in line with the demurely, conservatively dressed habitués and the shorts-clad (but jacket-and-tie sporting, as per the restaurant's official dress code) "Go-Cup" slurping tourists. Chatting lazily in the August swelter, for in Louisiana summer temperatures often reach 90°F, we were finally admitted into the cool, crystal- and white linen-fitted main dining room. Ordering was a dilemma: most of the dishes had French or partially French names; we wanted to concentrate on Louisiana food. Susan's father, an amateur of traditional French cuisine explained that while the names and the original recipes were indeed French, ingredients were

local and the technique of cooking was that of the early 1900s, when the restaurant was founded. The result was, therefore, totally different from what you'd be served in a Parisian restaurant. And as promised, despite recognizable components, the results were as far from any French cuisine we had tasted as they were from anything American we had ever experienced. There is a gentleness about the layered combinations of butter, herbs, and spices in the food and the tenderness of flesh and hints of sweet background flavors conjure an image of an ephemeral and fated "Old South." These somehow transform the familiar into the exotic.

# Creole Recipes

## Oysters Rockefeller

YIELDS 24 LARGE OYSTERS

This recipe originated at Antoine's restaurant in New Orleans around the turn of the century and was named for the Rockefeller family because it is so deliciously rich. Count three to six oysters per person, depending on the rest of the menu.

Open the oysters and remove them from their shells. Reserve in the refrigerator in their liquor. Wash the bottom part of the shells and place them on a ½-inch bed of coarse salt, on an oven- or broiler-proof pan.

The sauce should be made at least 1 hour and up to a day in advance. Wash the spinach and steam briefly with just the water clinging to the leaves. Squeeze to remove excess water. In a large skillet or wide saucepan, melt the butter and sweat the onions, scallion, celery, and garlic without coloring, for 2 to 3 minutes. Add the cooked spinach and mix until the sauce bubbles. Sprinkle with the flour and continue cooking 2 minutes. Add the cream and cook just until the sauce thickens. Add the Pernod, Worcestershire, Louisiana hot sauce, salt, and spices, and cook 5 minutes more. Allow to cool, and then refrigerate if not using within an hour.

Preheat the oven to 450°F. Replace the oysters in their cleaned shells on the bed of coarse salt. Mound each oyster with 1 or 2 tablespoons of the sauce. Sprinkle with a little parmesan. When the oven is up to temperature, bake the oysters for 6 to 10 minutes, just until the sauce is bubbling and golden. Prepare individual serving plates or a platter in advance, covered with seaweed or coarse salt to hold the hot shells upright. Remove the shells from the baking dish with caution — they're hot! — and place them on the plates or platter.

24 large oysters
2 pounds coarse salt
2 pounds fresh spinach, washed and stemmed
4 tablespoons butter
½ onion, finely chopped
1 whole scallion, or the white or light green part of a leek (1 ½ inches), finely chopped
½ celery stalk, finely chopped
2 garlic cloves, minced
1 tablespoon all-purpose flour
¾ cup crème fraîche or heavy cream
3 tablespoons Pernod or Herbsaint
1 tablespoon Worcestershire sauce
1 teaspoon Louisiana hot sauce or tabasco
½ teaspoon salt
½ teaspoon ground white pepper
¼ teaspoon ground cayenne pepper
grated parmesan for broiling

# Crab-Stuffed Mushrooms

As a cocktail appetizer or on a buffet table, use finger-sized mushrooms. For an appetizer served at the table, decide on the quantity per person proportion to the size of mushrooms available. If possible, use beige mushrooms — slightly firmer than the white and with the flavor of forest mushrooms.

Preheat the oven to 400°F. Remove the mushroom stems, discarding the sandy ends. Save the middle part to use in the stuffing. Wipe the mushroom heads with a kitchen or paper towel and place them on a baking dish. If they are not steady, cut a sliver off the head of the mushroom to stabilize it during cooking. Mound the stuffing in the opening, rounding it to follow the natural curve of the mushroom. Drizzle a little olive oil on the stuffing and bake for 6 to 10 minutes, until the tops are golden.

$\frac{1}{2}$ onion, finely chopped
$\frac{1}{2}$ green bell pepper, finely chopped
1 small celery stalk, finely chopped
2 small garlic cloves, minced
mushroom, eggplant, or artichoke trimmings
4 tablespoons butter

**Spice Mix**
$\frac{1}{2}$ teaspoon celery salt
$\frac{1}{4}$ teaspoon ground cayenne pepper
$\frac{1}{4}$ teaspoon ground white pepper
$\frac{1}{4}$ teaspoon ground sage

8 ounces crabmeat
1 egg, lightly beaten
8 tablespoons fine corn bread crumbs

# Crab Stuffing

YIELDS 2 CUPS OF STUFFING, ENOUGH FOR 12 TO 20 MUSHROOMS, 4 TO 6 PIROGUES, OR 10 TO 12 ARTICHOKE BOTTOMS, DEPENDING ON THE SIZE OF THE VEGETABLE.

**For Crab-Stuffed Mushrooms (above), Pirogues (page 94), and Eggs Sardou (page 55), cook the mushroom stems, the extra eggplant flesh, or the artichoke trimmings with the other vegetables at the beginning of the recipe.**

Sauté the onion, bell pepper, celery, garlic, and other vegetable trimmings in the butter with the spice mix. Once the vegetables are lightly colored, add the crabmeat and cook until uniformly golden. Allow to cool. Add the egg and corn bread crumbs. Refrigerate for 1 hour to 1 day before using to allow the corn bread to bind the other ingredients.

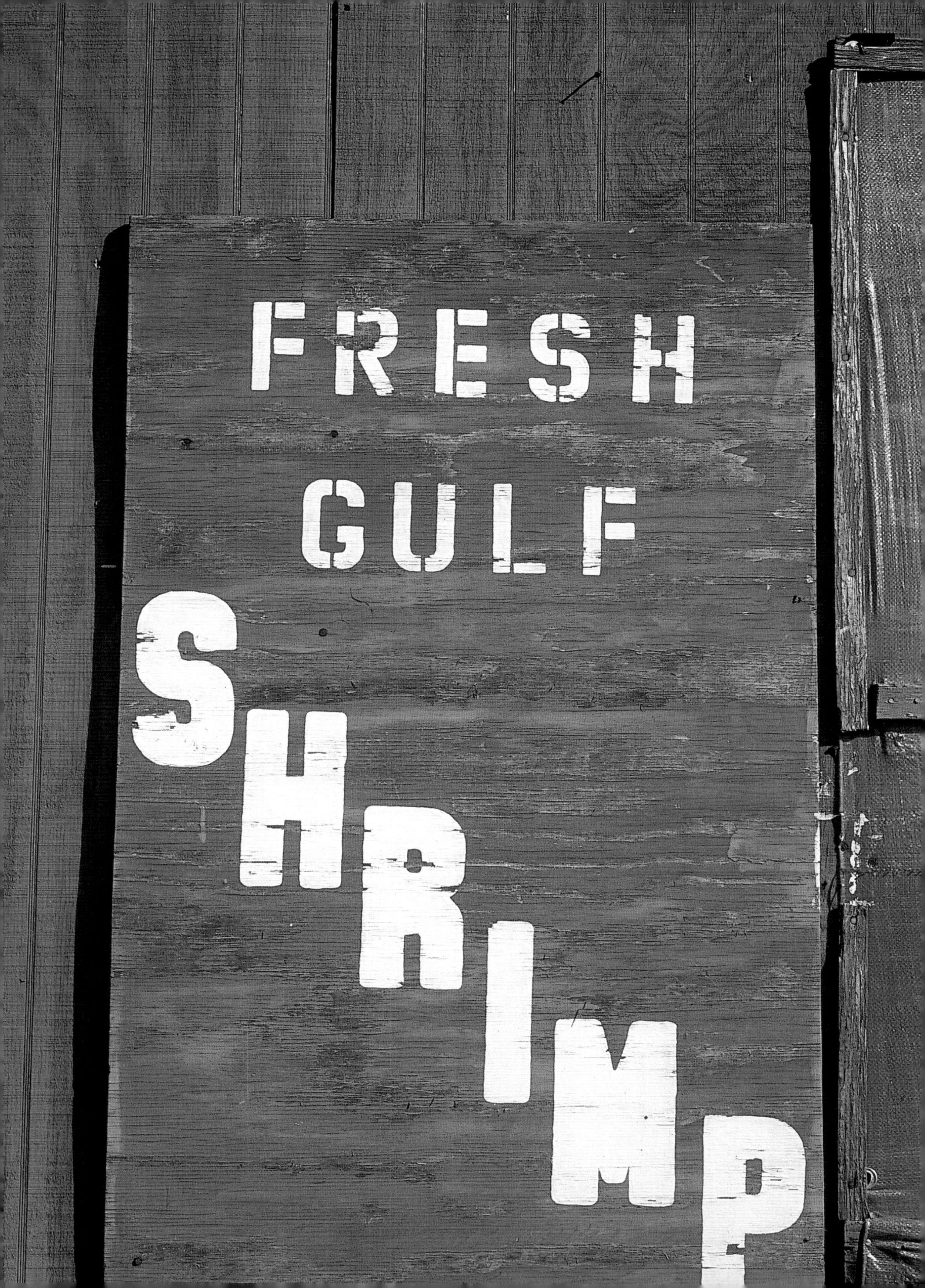
FRESH
GULF
SHRIMP

4 to 6 large shrimp or prawns per person

4 tablespoons lemon juice

1 medium onion, finely chopped

2 whole scallions, chopped

1 large or two small celery stalks, chopped

5 tablespoons prepared horseradish

6 tablespoons Dijon mustard

$^3/_4$ cup ketchup

1 tablespoon minced fresh parsley

$^1/_2$ teaspoon ground cayenne pepper

1 tablespoon Louisiana Gold Hot Sauce

$^1/_4$ teaspoon salt

$^1/_4$ teaspoon ground white pepper

1 cup vegetable oil

# Shrimp Remoulade

SERVES 6 TO 8

**Louisiana remoulade sauce is very different than its French predecessor. This recipe is also delicious with crab claws, crawfish tails, or as a simple dip for crudités.**

Defrost shrimp if frozen. In a large pot, bring 2 to 3 quarts of unsalted water to a boil and cook the whole shrimp 3 to 5 minutes, just until pink and firm. Cool the shrimp by plunging them into a bowl of ice water.

Put all ingredients except the shrimp and the vegetable oil in the bowl of a food processor, and pulse off and on a few minutes until the ingredients are well mixed but not liquified. Using the feed tube, add the vegetable oil while mixing. The sauce should be homogenous but not smooth; the vegetables should be a bit crunchy.

Shell the cooled shrimp, leaving the tail ends attached. Toss the heads and peelings back

into the cooking water and boil 20 minutes to make a stock for future use if desired (page 27).

To serve, hold the shrimp by the tail end and dip into the sauce to cover the shrimp completely and generously except for the tail end "handle." Place the shrimp carefully on a mixture of shredded lettuces or on cucumber rounds, either on individual plates or a large platter. Spoon a little extra sauce over all.

# Oyster and Spinach Soup with Parmesan Lace

SERVES 6

Open the oysters, reserving their juice. Strain the juice to remove any shell particles and refrigerate. Cover the oysters with water and refrigerate. In a large pot, melt the butter and sweat the onion and celery, without letting them color. Add the spices and bay leaves and cook 5 minutes. Add half of the Pernod and the garlic and cook another 2 minutes. Add the potato cubes and the stock and boil, partially covered, for 20 minutes. Crush the potatoes into the soup with a potato masher or the back of a large spoon. Add the cream, the filtered oyster juice, and the leeks and simmer, uncovered, for 10 minutes.

If you prefer a thicker soup, mix 4 table-spoons of cornstarch in the remainder of the Pernod and add slowly to the soup with the Worcestershire sauce and the parmesan and cook for 8 minutes. (Otherwise, just omit the cornstarch and add the rest.) Just before serving, poach the oysters and the spinach strips in the simmering soup for 3 minutes. Remove the oysters, place 4 in each individual bowl, and ladle in the soup. Garnish with 2 Parmesan Lace chips per serving.

## PARMESAN LACE

I have a small, cheap Teflon crepe pan that I use only for cheese lace. Have your grated cheese ready, preheat the pan until very hot, and sprinkle the cheese one tablespoon at a time on the hot surface of the pan in a very fine layer, in an oval shape about 1 x 2 inches. When the cheese is uniformly bubbling, remove the pan from the heat and allow to cool for 1 to 2 minutes. Gently lift off the cheese lace with a plastic spatula, and allow to cool on a wire rack. Once completely cooled, the lace keeps a week or two in an airtight container.

---

24 large oysters with their liquor

4 tablespoons butter

1 large onion, finely chopped

2 celery stalks, finely chopped

$\frac{1}{2}$ tablespoon salt

$\frac{1}{2}$ teaspoon ground white pepper

$\frac{1}{4}$ teaspoon ground cayenne pepper

3 bay leaves

$\frac{1}{2}$ cup Pernod, in all

1 large or 2 small garlic cloves, minced

2 cups peeled baking potatoes, chopped in cubes

2 quarts fish stock

1 cup heavy cream

1 leek, white and light green part only, cut in fine strips

4 tablespoons cornstarch (optional)

$\frac{1}{2}$ teaspoon Worchestershire sauce

4 tablespoons of grated parmesan + 12 tablespoons for the lace

7 ounces fresh spinach leaves, cut in fine strips

# Barbecue Shrimp

YIELDS 1 MAIN-COURSE SERVING

This is a favorite dish to eat outdoors in one of the cafés near the French Market in New Orleans, listening to live music and drinking Abita beer, a local brew difficult to find outside of Louisiana. In Paris, we serve it with herbed basmati rice; in New Orleans, extra bread is provided to soak up the delicious sauce.

You will need a pan with sides or a skillet that can stand a very hot oven and is large enough to accommodate the shrimp in a single layer. The measurements of ingredients are approximate and given per person as a guide.

Preheat the oven until very hot — 400°F. Place the lemon slices on the bottom of the baking dish, and place the defrosted shrimp, head and shell attached, in one layer on top of the lemon. Cover with all of the other ingredients in the order listed. Bake 10 to 12 minutes, just until the shrimp are cooked. To serve, remove the shrimp with tongs and place on a serving platter or on individual plates. Pour the sauce over the shrimp and serve with rice or crusty bread.

---

3 slices of lemon

6 to 8 whole shrimp or prawns

3 tablespoons garlic-infused olive oil

1 tablespoon Worchestershire sauce

$\frac{1}{2}$ teaspoon sea salt

1 teaspoon dried oregano

3 tablespoons crushed black pepper (enough to cover the shrimp — it seems like a lot but it's necessary)

4 tablespoons butter, cut in small cubes

# Plantation Chicken

SERVES 6 TO 8

**This recipe is more Creole than Cajun, and more modern than classical. It's very elegant served with steamed buttered spinach and wild rice.**

Crush each garlic glove and discard the peel. Remove the needles from a large rosemary sprig and reserve the other sprigs for the infusion. Mix together all of the components of the marinade.

Place the chicken parts skin side up in a baking dish large enough to accommodate them in a single layer and sprinkle with the salt and pepper. Pour the marinade over the chicken and verify that all parts are covered. Cover with plastic wrap and let marinate 8 hours or overnight in the refrigerator.

Preheat the oven to 350°F. On top of the stove, bring the chicken stock to a boil and add the rosemary. Allow to infuse off the heat while the chicken cooks.

Pour the white wine into the baking dish and cover the chicken with the brown sugar or brush with the honey. Bake uncovered, basting every 10 minutes with accumulated juices, for 45 minutes or until the chicken is cooked and golden.

**Acadian Village in Lafayette.**

About 10 minutes before the chicken has finished cooking, remove the rosemary from the chicken stock and boil to reduce a little. When the chicken is cooked, remove from the baking dish with the prunes and olives and keep warm. Deglaze the baking dish with the hot rosemary infusion, scraping with a whisk to get all the yummy brown bits stuck onto the baking dish. Simmer a few minutes to concentrate the flavor, and strain if you wish. Add a pinch of salt to taste and serve immediately poured over the chicken or passed in a sauce boat.

**The Marinade**
1 head of garlic
1 bunch fresh rosemary
$3/4$ cup olive oil
4 tablespoons raspberry vinegar
4 tablespoons dried oregano
4 bay leaves
1 cup green olives, pitted
4 tablespoons tiny capers, with a bit of juice
2 prunes per person
salt to taste

1 free-range chicken cut into 8, or 8 breast halves on the bone
2 tablespoons sea salt
1 tablespoon crushed black pepper
2 cups strong chicken stock
$1/2$ cup white wine
1 cup packed dark brown sugar (preferred), or $1/2$ cup honey

# Pirogue Bayou Teche

SERVES 8

**Spice Mix**

2 tablespoons paprika

1 tablespoon salt

1 tablespoon onion powder

1 tablespoon garlic powder

1 tablespoon herbs de Provence

2 teaspoons ground white pepper

2 teaspoons ground cayenne pepper

**For the Sauce**

1 cup vegetable oil

1 cup all-purpose flour

$\frac{1}{2}$ onion, finely chopped

1 small celery stalk, finely chopped

$\frac{1}{2}$ green bell pepper, finely chopped

6 cups shrimp stock (preferred)
or fish stock, heated

4 small eggplants

1 recipe Crab Stuffing (page 86)

24 large shrimp or prawns

1 beaten egg

1 cup milk

vegetable oil for deep-frying

2 cups all-purpose flour

2 cups bread crumbs

In the past as well as the present, Cajuns used the small wooden boats called pirogues to navigate the bayous, to fish, crab, or gather oysters, or just to commune with nature. The region around Bayou Teche was the first settlement of Acadians in Louisiana.

The Bayou Teche sauce can be made a day in advance, and reheated. Please read "First Make a Roux..." before starting (page 22).

Mix the ingredients in the spice mix together and reserve. In a large, heavy-bottomed pot, heat the oil until very hot, and add the flour, whisking constantly until the roux is the color of milk chocolate. Lower the heat or remove the pot during this process if necessary to avoid burning the roux. Once the roux is the desired color, remove from or lower the heat and carefully add the vegetables and 1 tablespoon of the spice mix. This will produce a lot of very hot steam, so keep your face well away from the pot. Continue mixing until the roux calms a bit, then return it to the heat and incorporate the hot stock ladle by ladle, stirring and keeping the sauce at a constant slow boil. Simmer slowly for 15 minutes and strain. Let cool before refrigerating if made in advance; if continuing with the recipe, set the sauce aside in its pot.

## FOR THE PIROGUES

Peel the eggplants and cut in half lengthwise. Placing each half cut-side up and using a small knife, cut a shallow line $\frac{1}{2}$ inch from the edge and following the perimeters of the eggplants. With a spoon remove the pulp from the center, leaving walls $\frac{1}{2}$ inch thick. Reserve this pulp for the Crab Stuffing (page 86). If the eggplant halves wobble when placed cut-side up, cut a fine slice off the bottom. The eggplants can be prepared up to this point a day in advance, and kept individually covered in the refrigerator.

Peel the shrimp. If you have the heads, save them to toss into the sauce while it's reheating — they lend a delicious flavor. Sauté the Crab Stuffing in a little butter until it's golden and slightly dry, and keep warm. Mix the egg with the milk in a bowl large enough to hold one eggplant half. Heat the frying oil at a depth of about 2 inches in a deep fryer or in a large heavy pot to 375°F.

Pat each half of the eggplant first with the spice mix, then dredge with the flour. Tap to remove excess flour, and dip the eggplant in the egg/milk mixture, coating well, then cover with the bread crumbs. Fry the eggplants, one or two at a time, turning once with tongs after about 3 minutes, until they are golden brown, about 6 minutes in all. Drain on absorbent paper. While the eggplants are frying, heat the Bayou Teche sauce and cook with the shrimp heads, if you have them. When the eggplants are all cooked, remove the shrimp heads from the sauce and poach the peeled tails, about three minutes, in the sauce.

To serve, fill each pirogue with Crab Stuffing and place on serving dish. Remove the cooked shrimp tails from the sauce and place 3 tails on the crab stuffing in each pirogue. Pour about $\frac{1}{4}$ cup of sauce over the shrimps on the eggplants. Serve with basmati rice.

# Snap Beans Soulant

SERVES 6

This recipe is a wonderful way to prepare green beans, which benefit from this unfashionably long cooking period. "Snap beans" is the Louisiana term for green beans so crispy that they "snap" when you break off the ends. Cook them in the morning and let them stand until dinner for maximum flavor.

Cut off the ends of the green beans and soak them in cold water while browning the bacon in a large skillet. Once the bacon is golden, add the onion and garlic, stirring so the vegetables don't burn. Add a little lard or vegetable oil if necessary. When the onions become transparent, drain the green beans and add to the pan. Cover, lower the heat to a minimum, and cook for at least one hour, until the green beans are tender.

While the green beans simmer, boil the potatoes in salted water just until tender when pierced by an inquiring knife point, then drain. When the green beans are cooked, add the potatoes to the pot and mix well. Before serving, sprinkle with sea salt and crushed black pepper.

2 pounds green beans
1 pound thick strip bacon, cut into $\frac{1}{2}$-inch pieces
1 large onion, finely chopped
2 garlic cloves, minced
lard or vegetable oil
$\frac{1}{2}$ pound small fingerling potatoes, washed and unpeeled
sea salt and crushed black pepper

# Louisiana Crab Cakes

YIELDS 8 CRAB CAKES

Crab cakes are popular in all regions that harvest crabs, particularly the southeastern shore from Maryland down around Florida and west to Louisiana. Louisiana crab cakes are spicier than other versions, but just enough to accentuate the delicate flavor of crabmeat. If you have the patience to pick it out, the meat from freshly cooked king crab legs, or stone or Dungeness crab, is divine. Otherwise, use the best-quality frozen or canned crab you can find.

In a large bowl, mix the crab (if there are some large pieces, don't break them all up), the vegetables, and the dry spices. In a smaller bowl, beat the eggs with the mustard, the Worchestershire, and the hot sauce, and add to the crab mixture. Add 6 tablespoons of bread crumbs and mix well with your hands. Let sit 5 minutes. If the mixture is too soft to form patties, add a little more bread crumbs and wait another 5 minutes. Make 8 patties of 2 to 3 inches in diameter with a good $\frac{1}{2}$-inch thickness. Pour the rest of the bread crumbs into a bowl and one by one, drop in the crab cakes and coat them with the bread crumbs, pressing lightly. Allow to rest at least 5 minutes and up to $\frac{1}{2}$ hour before frying.

Heat $\frac{1}{2}$ inch of vegetable oil in a heavy, nonstick frying pan. Without crowding the pan, fry the crab cakes until crispy and golden, about 5 minutes on each side. If you're frying in batches, the cooked crab cakes can be kept warm and crispy in a preheated warm oven 200°F.
Serve with Tartar Sauce (page 151) and Cajun Potato Salad (page 115).

1 pound crabmeat
$\frac{1}{2}$ celery stalk, minced
$\frac{1}{2}$ green bell pepper, finely chopped
$\frac{1}{2}$ onion, minced
$\frac{1}{2}$ teaspoon celery salt
$\frac{1}{4}$ teaspoon ground white pepper
$\frac{1}{4}$ teaspoon ground cayenne pepper
2 eggs
1 tablespoon Dijon mustard
2 teaspoons Worchestershire sauce
1 teaspoon Louisiana hot sauce
2 cups bread crumbs
vegetable oil for frying

# Cajun Country

Southwest of New Orleans, along the Bayou Teche in Breaux Bridge, the heart of the Cajun country, Rocky's Bayou Boudin & Cracklin Café is installed in a whitewashed, picket fence–enclosed house. French-style and Zydeco accordions, harmonicas, stuffed alligator heads, and crawfish-printed bandannas decorate the walls beside posters announcing regional fêtes and framed photographs of local winners of accordion and Cajun dance contests. Cajun, Zydeco, and country music wafts through the café. Wooden tables with mismatched chairs seat up to twenty or so habitués and cabin guests; during a busy daily lunch service the predominant language is Cajun French, and the predominant meal is, yes, homemade boudin and cracklins.

Cajun French is essentially a patois based on eighteenth-century French seasoned with a pinch of Spanish, Native American, African, and English; automobiles are *chars*, shrimp are *chevrettes*, and a dollar is a *piastre*. The principal language of southwest Louisiana until 1912, when Governor Hall banned the speaking of French in public school, it has recently enjoyed a renaissance due to the pride and determination of the Acadian people to preserve their culture, or *lache pas la patate*. Cajun Boudin Blanc is a mostly pork-and-rice stuffed sausage with spices and other ingredients that vary from cook to cook. Served with a roux-based gravy and either potatoes or rice, it is a regional staple, either homemade or store-bought. Cracklins are fried pieces of pork rind, which can be nibbled like potato chips. Also on the menu is an excellent Crawfish Etouffée, Dirty Rice, and Chicken Gumbo with

**Preceding spread: Giant crawfish at Breaux Bridge, crawfish capital of the world.**
**Left: Cajun Boudin Blanc (page 105).**
**Above: Conrad Rice Cooperative in New Iberia.**

a hard-boiled egg cooked right in it. Coffee is kept steaming hot in an urn by the cash register; you serve yourself. Hogs head cheese, tasso ham (a Cajun smoked and spiced ham available only in Louisiana), andouille sausages, and Rocky's homemade Cajun pralines are sold from a take-out counter at the back of the café. Outdoors, guarded by a gargantuan metal sculpted crawfish, a 1940s bait shop tilts precariously on 6-foot stilts, soon to be transformed into one of Rocky's guest cabins. Under a nearby oak is the 50-gallon *chaudière* (cast-iron pot) that Rocky uses to cook his boudin and fry his cracklins, beginning at 5 A.M. every day but Sunday.

**Above: Acadian Village in Lafayette.**
**Right: Craft machine at Acadian Village.**

# Cajun Recipes

## Cajun Boudin Blanc

YIELDS 10 SAUSAGES OF ABOUT
12 INCHES IN LENGTH EACH

If you don't have access to a sausage stuffer, you can stuff the sausage casings using a funnel while the mixture is warm. Or you can allow the mixture to solidify in the refrigerator and make sausage patties.

In a wide, large pot, mix the lean and fatty ground pork, cream, water, onion, garlic, scallions, and parsley and cook over a medium heat, stirring often until the meat is cooked, around 15 minutes. Add the ground poultry and rice, mixing well. Turn off the heat and add the spice mix, mixing well. Let stand 30 minutes, stirring from time to time. If you are stuffing sausage casings, do it now; if you're making patties, refrigerate uncovered until cold and solid before forming the patties. In either case, let the formed sausages rest in the refrigerator a few hours to 2 days before serving.

To serve, brown the boudins on both sides in a little lard or vegetable oil. If in sausage casings, they will partially explode; just remove them and their deliciously crusty fallout with a spatula and place them on individual serving plates. Cover with Brown Beer and Juniper Berry Sauce (below), and accompany with Smashed Potatoes (page 72) or Duck Dirty Rice (page 38).

1 pound lean ground pork

1 pound fatty ground pork

1 cup crème fraîche or heavy cream

$3/4$ cup water

1 onion, finely chopped

1 tablespoon minced garlic

2 whole scallions or the white and light green part of a leek, chopped

4 tablespoons chopped parsley

1 pound leftover cooked chicken or turkey, ground or finely chopped

3 cups cooked rice

**Spice Mix**

2 tablespoons ground sage

$1\frac{1}{4}$ tablespoons salt

1 tablespoon herbes de Provence

1 teaspoon ground white pepper

1 teaspoon cayenne pepper

1 teaspoon allspice

$1/2$ teaspoon ground bay leaves

## Brown Beer and Juniper Berry Sauce

YIELDS APPROXIMATELY 1 QUART

Heat the stock and set aside. In a heavy-bottomed casserole, heat the fat or oil until very hot and add the flour, stirring constantly with a whisk over medium heat. Be careful not to burn it. (Read "First Make a Roux...," page 22.) When the roux is the color of milk chocolate, lower the heat to a minimum and slowly incorporate the hot stock, ladle by ladle, whisking. This will produce steam, so be careful. Add the bay leaves and allow to boil slowly for 10 minutes, then add the brown beer, juniper berries, salt and pepper, and thyme. Cook 15 to 20 minutes more. The sauce should have the consistency of heavy cream. If it's too thin, continue cooking a bit; if it's too thick, add a little liquid.

1 quart chicken stock

$1/2$ cup chicken fat or vegetable oil, or a mixture of the two

$1/2$ cup all-purpose flour

4 bay leaves

$1/2$ bottle or can of brown beer

2 tablespoons juniper berries

$1/2$ teaspoon salt

$1/2$ teaspoon ground white pepper

1 tablespoon thyme

**Left: Dining room at the Laura Plantation in Vacherie.**

11 pounds large live crawfish
6 carrots, sliced in rounds
6 onions, sliced in rings
4 celery stalks, cut into ½-inch pieces,
leaves reserved
one head of garlic, cloves peeled and crushed
1 whole leek, cut into ½-inch pieces
olive oil
10 bay leaves
1 bunch of parsley
a few sprigs of thyme
1 tablespoon black peppercorns
about 1 gallon crab, fish, or vegetable stock,
diluted with an equal quantity of water
to make 2 gallons
1 tablespoon Louisiana hot sauce per person
3 tablespoons coarse salt
2 pounds tiny fingerling potatoes, washed,
with their skins
5 ears of corn, cut into thirds

1 green bell pepper, finely chopped
1 long or 2 small celery stalks, finely chopped
1 large or 2 small onions, finely chopped
2 to 3 garlic cloves, minced
5 tablespoons butter

**Spice Mix**
1 teaspoon celery salt
½ teaspoon cayenne pepper
¼ teaspoon ground white pepper

1 small can (10 ounces) of crushed tomatoes,
drained, but with the juice reserved
1 pound crawfish tails, peeled
4 tablespoons chopped parsley
4 tablespoons all-purpose flour
1 cup liquid (the juice reserved from the
tomatoes plus some stock or water if necessary)

# Crawfish Boil

SERVES 8 TO 10

It's a bit of Cajun lore that the Atlantic lobsters so missed the Acadians when they fled Nova Scotia in 1785 that they followed them to Louisiana. But the trip was so long and arduous that those who survived lost so much weight that they became crawfish. Crawfish are abundant in Louisiana from October through May; they are sold live, steamed, or boiled. Out of season they can be purchased whole, cooked, and frozen in the shell, or you can buy just the frozen tailmeat, which is perfect for Crawfish Étouffée.

Pick through the crawfish and discard any corpses. The majority of crawfish now on the market are farmed; therefore, it's no longer necessary to remove the sand tract before cooking. Reserve them in a cold, dark place covered with a damp towel.

In a large pot (a lobster pot is ideal) sauté half of the pieces of carrot, onions, and celery with all of the garlic and leeks in just enough olive oil to coat the bottom of the pot. Cook about 10 minutes until soft and golden. Add the herbs and the peppercorns, then the stock and the water, and bring to a boil. Add half of the hot sauce and half of the salt. Allow to simmer uncovered for 30 minutes, strain, and discard the cooked veggies; pour the strained liquid back into the pot. Taste, and add the rest of the hot sauce and the salt if necessary; the liquid should be very spicy and salty. Bring back to a boil, add the potatoes, and cook 10 minutes. Add the pieces of corn and the rest of the reserved veggies, including the celery leaves. Boil 10 minutes, remove all the vegetables with a large slotted spoon, and reserve. When the liquid is at a hard boil, cook about one quarter of the crawfish, checking that they are covered by the boiling liquid as they cook. After about 5 minutes, when they have become bright red, remove the crawfish with a long-handled slotted spoon and reserve. Repeat until all the crawfish are cooked. To serve, layer the crawfish and the veggies in a large dish, pour the hot liquid over them, and allow each guest to serve himself. Expect 12 to 15 crawfish per person.

# Crawfish Étouffée

YIELDS 4 MAIN-COURSE PORTIONS
OR 8 APPETIZERS

Crawfish tails smothered in a spicy sauce, this dish is traditionally served as a main course with white rice. In smaller portions, it also makes an unusual appetizer.

In a wide pot or a large frying pan with high sides, sweat the bell pepper, celery, onion, and garlic in the butter for 8 minutes. Add the spice mix and the drained tomatoes and simmer for 6 minutes. Add the crawfish tails and the parsley and cook another 4 minutes, stirring from time to time. Add the flour to the 1 cup of liquid, stirring with a whisk to prevent lumps, then add to the pan. Cook another 2 to 4 minutes, just until the sauce thickens.

Serve with basmati rice or angel hair pasta.

# Southern Fried Chicken

6 SERVINGS

Drumsticks are great for this recipe because they're easy to eat with your hands, but you can use other chicken parts as well. If you have a deep fryer, follow the manufacturer's directions; if not, a wide, heavy-bottomed skillet with high sides will do the trick. Fill it with a scant inch of vegetable oil. You will need tongs to turn the chicken while frying and to remove the finished pieces.

Rub the chicken pieces with the spice rub and let sit at room temperature for 30 minutes. Beat the eggs in a large bowl and whisk in the milk. Heat the oil to 375°F. Dip the chicken pieces one by one in the egg mixture, then roll them in the flour. Shake off the excess and plunge them into the hot oil, one at a time. For crispy results, it's important that the oil be the correct temperature. Don't crowd the fryer; you will have better results frying in 2 batches than trying to cook the chicken all at once. If you're frying in a skillet, turn the pieces after 5 or 6 minutes. Fry a total of 10 to 15 minutes, depending on the size of the pieces, until the chicken is a deep golden brown. Drain on paper towels. If you're frying in batches, the chicken can be kept warm and crispy in a 200°F oven, uncovered, while you're frying the rest.

Serve with Smashed Potatoes (page 72), Cole Slaw (page 110), and Corn Bread (page 149).

**Spice Rub**
1 tablespoon salt
2 tablespoons herbes de Provence
1 tablespoon garlic powder
1 tablespoon ground cayenne pepper

12 drumsticks or other pieces of chicken
2 beaten eggs
2 cups whole milk
vegetable oil for frying
1 pound all-purpose flour

# Barbecue Ribs

SERVES 4 TO 5

There are hundreds of styles of barbecue sauce in the South and many different ways to cook ribs: boiled, baked, or grilled outdoors, for instance. Homemade sauces take hours to cook and aren't always the correct consistency to stick to the meat. I prefer a sauce that adheres well to baked or grilled ribs, and have developed this method of cooking them using a store-bought barbecue sauce and a home oven. You will need an ovenproof pan with sides to capture the juices, and a pair of tongs to handle the meat.

Cut the ribs apart, leaving an equal amount of meat on each side of the bone. Marinate the ribs in the liquid smoke a few hours in the refrigerator.

Preheat the oven to 375°F. Place the ribs, bone-side down, in an ovenproof baking dish with at least a $\frac{1}{2}$-inch rim. Sprinkle with salt and pepper. Cook 20 minutes.

Remove the pan from the oven and discard the baking juices. Turn the ribs one by one with tongs so that the bone side is facing up. Cook another 20 minutes.

Remove the pan from the oven and discard the juices (it is nearly all fat, so don't pour it down the sink!). Empty the barbecue sauce into a bowl and, using the tongs, dip each rib into the sauce, shake off the excess, and return to the baking dish, bone-side down. Cook another 15 to 20 minutes, just until the ribs are lightly caramelized. Serve with Cole Slaw (page 110), Cajun Potato Salad (page 115), and Corn Bread (page 149).

2 racks of pork ribs
(about 4 $\frac{1}{2}$ pounds, 24 ribs total)
4 tablespoons liquid smoke
salt and pepper to taste
1 bottle of a good store-bought barbecue sauce

**The Veggies**

1 head of cabbage, chopped in fine strips

1 large or 2 small onions, chopped

1 green bell pepper, chopped in small cubes

1 red bell pepper, chopped in small cubes

2 carrots, grated

2 tablespoons cumin seeds

**The Marinade**

1 cup cider vinegar

$\frac{1}{2}$ cup water

$\frac{1}{2}$ cup vegetable oil

4 tablespoons sugar

1 teaspoon salt

1 teaspoon ground white pepper

1 tablespoon Dijon mustard

2 cups Basic Mayonnaise (page 115)

# Cole Slaw

YIELDS ABOUT 10 CUPS

Mix all of the veggies with the cumin seeds in a large bowl. In a saucepan, mix all of the marinade ingredients with a whisk and bring to a boil. Pour the hot marinade over the vegetables and let sit 30 minutes at room temperature. Add the mayonnaise and mix well. Allow to marinate in the refrigerator for at least 2 hours before serving. Cole Slaw can be made a day or two in advance; it improves in the refrigerator.

# Cajun Meatloaf

SERVES 6 TO 8

Preheat the oven to 350°F.

In a large bowl, mix the meats, spices, eggs, bread crumbs, onion, garlic and one-third of the ketchup with your hands. Form a compact loaf about 10 x 4 inches in or on an ovenproof dish. With a brush or the back of a spoon, paint the meatloaf with half the ketchup, and sprinkle with 1 tablespoon of the herbes de Provence. Bake 45 minutes.

Remove the meatloaf from the oven. Paint with the remaining ketchup and sprinkle with the remaining tablespoon of herbes de Provence. Cook for another 15 minutes. Allow to rest for 10 to 20 minutes before slicing.

This meatloaf is also delicious cold, and makes wonderful sandwiches with ketchup, pickles, and slices of red onion. Try it on onion rolls.

$1\frac{1}{2}$ pounds ground beef

$\frac{3}{4}$ pound ground pork

**Spice Mix**

2 teaspoons cayenne pepper

1 teaspoon ground pepper

1 teaspoon paprika

1 tablespoon salt

1 tablespoon herbes de Provence

1 tablespoon ground cumin

2 eggs

1 cup bread crumbs

1 onion, chopped

2 cloves of garlic, minced

$1\frac{1}{2}$ cups ketchup

2 tablespoons herbes de Provence for decoration

# Cajun Cabin Pie

SERVES 10

Variations of ground meat and mashed-potato pies are found in nearly all cultures: the Greek moussaka, the Irish shepherd's pie, and the French hachis parmentier. This Cajun version is a riot of color, textures, and flavor.

Preheat the oven to 400°F. While beginning to prepare the rest of this recipe, bake the sweet potatoes or yams in their skins, 1 hour or until soft. When they're cooked, let them rest just until they are cool enough to remove the skins. Mash the pulp with the 3 1/2 tablespoons of butter and the nutmeg with a potato masher or a large fork.

In an 8 x 10 x 2-inch baking dish, mix the ground meats with the eggs and bread crumbs. In a skillet, sauté the onion, celery, green pepper, and garlic in the butter. Add the meat seasoning mix, Worcestershire sauce, and Louisiana hot sauce and cook about 5 minutes, stirring often and scraping the bottom of the pan. Add the heavy cream and mix well, scraping all of the particles off the bottom of the pan. Allow to cool a few minutes, then add it to the meat mixture,

incorporating well with your hands. Press into the baking dish; it should form a loaf of about 1 to 1 1/2-inches) high. Bake at 400°F for about 20 minutes, until the meat is lightly browned. (It can share the oven with the yams.)

While the meats and yams are baking, sauté the carrots and remaining onion in the olive oil and butter. Cook about 5 minutes, then add the vegetable seasoning mix, peppers, and zucchini. Cook another five minutes, scraping the bottom of the skillet. Remove the skillet from the heat and set aside. When the meat is cooked, pour its accumulated drippings into the skillet with the vegetables, and cook 3 minutes over a high heat. Set aside.

Raise the oven temperature to 450°F. Spread half of the vegetable mixture with its juices over the meat, then spread on the yam purée. Spread the rest of the vegetable mixture on the yams, and finish by spreading the hot (or reheated) Smashed Potatoes over the veggies. Sprinkle with the parmesan and bake 15 to 20 minutes, just until golden and hot. Allow to rest 10 minutes before slicing.

2 pounds orange sweet potatoes or yams
3 1/2 tablespoons butter, cut in small cubes
1/2 teaspoon nutmeg
1 1/2 pounds ground beef
1/2 pound ground pork
2 eggs
1/2 cup bread crumbs
1 onion, chopped
1 large celery stalk, diced
1 green bell pepper, diced
2 garlic cloves, minced
3 1/2 tablespoons butter
1 tablespoon Worcestershire sauce
1 teaspoon Louisiana hot sauce
4 tablespoons heavy cream

**Meat Seasoning Mix**
2 teaspoons ground cayenne pepper
2 teaspoons salt
1 teaspoon pepper
1 teaspoon ground cumin
1 tablespoon herbes de Provence

2 carrots, cut in fine strips
1 onion, sliced in fine rounds
1/3 cup olive oil
3 1/2 tablespoons butter
1 red bell pepper, cut in fine strips
1 green bell pepper, cut in fine strips
1 zucchini, cut in 2-inch-long fine strips

**Vegetable Seasoning Mix**
1/2 teaspoon salt
1/4 teaspoon ground white pepper
1/4 teaspoon ground cayenne pepper
2 tablespoons dried basil

1/2 recipe of Smashed Potatoes, about 2 pounds
(page 72, leftovers are okay)
1/2 cup grated Parmesan

# Cajun Chili Con Carne

SERVES 8 TO 10

Soak the beans overnight in double their volume of water. To cook, boil them in salted water with a few bay leaves about 1 hour, until they are al dente. Drain and reserve; they will finish cooking in the chili.

Mix the spices. Cut the meat into 1/2-inch cubes and chop the onion and garlic by hand or in a food processor. Brown the meat over high heat in a little vegetable oil in a large, heavy-bottomed casserole, stirring often. When the meat has lost its raw look, add the onion and garlic, stirring frequently until they are colored and have rendered

their liquid. Add the spices, mix well, and cook an additional 5 minutes.

Add the canned tomatoes, the tomato paste, the water, and the wine. Bring to a boil, lower the heat, and simmer uncovered for about 3 hours, stirring every 20 minutes or so.

Add the cooked beans and simmer another 45 minutes, until the beans are tender. If the chili is too dry, add a little water. Serve in a large bowl accompanied by individual small bowls of grated cheddar, crème fraîche or sour cream, chopped onion, and cilantro.

20 ounces dry red kidney beans
bay leaves
8 tablespoons chili powder
1 tablespoon herbes de Provence
1 tablespoon ground cumin
1 tablespoon ground cayenne pepper
1 tablespoon salt
1/2 tablespoon ground white pepper
3 pounds beef
3 pounds onion, chopped
6 garlic cloves, minced
2 cups crushed tomatoes, with juice
3/4 cup tomato paste
1 quart water
1/2 bottle of red wine (about 1 1/2 cups)

**Left: Red Beans and Rice (page 41).**

# Cajun Potato Salad

Wash but don't peel the potatoes. Cut into uniform rounds of ¼-inch thick. Place the potatoes in a large pot of cold salted water, bring to a boil, and cook until tender, about 10 minutes. Do not overcook. Drain and rinse with cold water to stop the cooking. Allow to dry on a tea towel while preparing the rest.

Chop the eggs, and cut the scallions and celery into thin rounds. In a large bowl, layer them with the potatoes. Add the dill mayonnaise and turn gently. Before serving, sprinkle with the sea salt and crushed black pepper to taste.

2 pounds new red potatoes

4 hard-boiled eggs

2 whole scallions

1 celery stalk

1 recipe Basic Mayonnaise, flavored with ½ bunch of chopped dill

sea salt

crushed black pepper

## BASIC MAYONNAISE

YIELDS ABOUT 2 CUPS

Note that this recipe uses uncooked eggs, which may present the slight risk of a danger from salmonella bacteria. Adding an acid such as lemon juice or vinegar usually kills these bacteria as effectively as heat, but if you are nervous about this, use store-bought mayonnaise.

Place all of the ingredients except the oil in the bowl of a food processor and mix. Slowly add the oil through the feed tube while the processor is running. To flavor the mayonnaise with fresh herbs, mince them finely by hand and stir into the finished mayonnaise with a spoon.

2 egg yolks

1 whole egg

1 tablespoon prepared mustard

1 tablespoon lemon juice

½ teaspoon salt

½ teaspoon ground white pepper

2 cups vegetable oil

**Entranceway to Chretien Point Plantation at sunset.**

# Laisser les Bons Temps Rouler A Cajun Renaissance

The most important element in any cuisine is the quality and freshness of its components. In Paris, there is an abundance of garden-quality fruit and vegetables, free-range fowl, game, and seafood. Although at the restaurant we import several American essentials, such as filé powder, pecans, Karo syrup, and cornmeal, due to legislation, perishability, or prohibitive cost there are many specialties to which we don't have access: tasso ham, Louisiana andouille sausage, and blue crabs, to name a few. On the other hand, we can easily procure in France many products unavailable or difficult to get in American markets that were employed in Cajun home-cooking: crepines (the lacy animal stomach lining used for sausage-like preparations), frogs' legs, rabbit, gizzards, and all sorts of fats like duck, goose, or rendered pork fat.

And speaking of fat: all Southern, including Cajun, cuisines have a much-deserved reputation for being heavy, fatty, and unhealthy by modern standards. This is inherent to their character — cuisines developed in agrarian environments in rural areas of the South. While lightening up our recipes a bit, I continue to use duck, goose, or pork fat occasionally when it is necessary to the quality and identity of the dish. All three fats contain less cholesterol than butter, although of course, more than unhydrogenated vegetable oils.

**Preceding spread, left: Signs at Breaux Bridge.
Preceding spread, right: Accordian from
Mulate's restaurant.**

Although all of the recipes in this book were created in Paris, they are transformations of American recipes, some classic, some personal. Global marketing, for better or for worse, has made most specialty ingredients easily accessible worldwide. But it's fun, less expensive, and usually tastier to substitute fresh, local ingredients for imported. We use Montbeillard sausage for Cajun andouille sausage (which is not the same as French andouille), *rascasse* for redfish, and, often, the light green parts of leeks for scallions. (In France, leeks are easily available, while scallions are difficult to procure and rather expensive.) As in any family-style cuisine, there are nearly as many versions of each recipe as there are families, so do substitute local ingredients when necessary. If in Kansas you can't find preserved duck gizzards for Dirty Rice, use an artisanal wood-smoked bacon. If you're preparing Bayoubaisse along the coast of Massachusetts, by all means use the catch of the day. And wild

rice mixed with basmati makes an interesting contrast to garnish gumbos.

Cooking for a restaurant in some ways mirrors the hectic lifestyle most of us know today: so much to do and so little time in which to do it. Good organization and preparation — the famous *mis en place* — is the best time-saver there is. Cut all your veggies in advance, combine all your spices, and measure your rice, butter, flour, and oil before beginning to cook. That way everything is at hand and nothing burns while you chase the slippery and elusive garlic clove around the kitchen. Vegetables, as well as ham and other cooked meats, can be chopped the night before and stored, tightly covered, in the refrigerator. In restaurants, many dishes are completed up to a point, refrigerated, and finished on order, which often improves the final flavor. This can work at home, too, allowing you more time with your guests before the meal.

At the restaurant, our cuisine, and some of the recipes in this book, are not necessarily classical Cajun cuisine, if "classical" can ever describe a popular cuisine of such diverse influences. But they are typical in spirit, as

**Above: Antique plate warmer, Nottoway Plantation near White Castle.**

well as true to the basic cooking style and Cajun philosophy of extracting as much flavor from food — and life — as possible. In Paris, the abundance of prime-quality ingredients and the skill, creativity, and dedication of the many chefs and other restaurant personnel I've worked with make cooking a joy, even during frantic 14-hour workdays. And the interest and reaction of our French clientele to a new-world cuisine with historical and culinary links to their own — kind of like seeing grandfather's nose on the new baby's face — is rewarding in its own rite. Re-creating an ethnic cuisine outside of its region of origin is a balancing act, one which inspires creativity. And that is one of the things which assures the evolution and immortality of a culture.

The recipes that follow were developed in our restaurant kitchen with Cajun spirit and ingredients in mind, but with a nod toward the current trend to a fresh, lighter, and healthy cuisine. I refer to them as "Bayou la Seine" recipes, as we are located just two blocks from the Seine River in Paris, and they indeed represent a cross-pollination of flavor, technique, and style.

**Following spread:**
**Typical Bayou landscape.**

# Bayou la Seine

## CAJUN RECIPES "Made in France"

## Sweet Potato Soup with Rosemary and Pecans

SERVES 8

Heat the onion and the garlic in the butter in a large soup pot and sauté the onion and garlic over medium. Before they begin to brown, add the yams, cinnamon, star anise, and the stock. Remove the rosemary needles from their stems and reserve, tossing the stems into the pot. Raise the heat and bring to a boil; lower heat and simmer half covered for 20 minutes or until the yams are soft.

Remove the pot from the heat and discard the cinnamon sticks and the star anise. In a food processor, purée the soup in batches until smooth. Return the puréed soup to the pot, add the Spice Mix and the cream, and heat just to the boiling point. Taste and adjust the seasonings, if necessary. If the soup is too thick, add a bit of milk or stock.

To serve, garnish with the reserved rosemary needles, minced very fine, and the pecan pieces.

1 onion, finely chopped
3 garlic cloves, smashed
3 ½ tablespoons butter
2 pounds orange sweet potatoes or yams, peeled and cut into 1-inch rounds
2 cinnamon sticks
3 star anise
2 quarts chicken or vegetable stock
2 sprigs fresh rosemary

**Spice Mix**
½ teaspoon allspice
2 teaspoons ground ginger
1 teaspoon salt
½ teaspoon ground white pepper
½ teaspoon ground cinnamon
½ teaspoon ground nutmeg

¾ cup heavy cream
¼ cup pecans, chopped

## Roasted Onion and Garlic Soup

SERVES 6

**This soup is even better made a day in advance and reheated.**

Preheat the oven to 350°F. Remove the outer skins of the garlic heads, cut them in half widthwise, and plunge them into boiling water for 5 minutes. Remove the outer skins of the onions and shallots, cut them in four, and place them with the blanched garlic in a baking dish. Rub them with the olive oil, and sprinkle with sea salt and crushed black pepper. Roast for 1 to 1 ½ hours, stirring occasionally, until all the vegetables are soft and brown-tinged.

Remove the roasted veggies from the baking dish and deglaze the dish with the wine: while the dish is very hot, pour in the wine and scrape up all the browned particles with a whisk. Pour this liquid along with the vegetables and the stock into a large pot and bring to a boil. Lower the heat, cover, and simmer 1 hour. Pass through a food mill or purée in a food processor and strain. Taste and adjust the seasonings. If the soup is too thin, reduce it a little.

Garnish with chive sticks or Parmesan Lace (page 91).

½ pound garlic (3 or 4 heads)
1 pound onions, peeled
4 small shallots
4 tablespoons olive oil
sea salt
crushed black pepper
½ cup white wine
6 cups chicken or vegetable stock

**Patron at Mulate's restaurant in Breaux Bridge.**

# Bayoubaisse

SERVES 8

There are different versions of bouillabaisse in Louisiana, and most of them try very hard to be French. We wanted to develop a version redolent of the bayous, so we've used a fumet based on crab, an olive oil roux to bind the soup, and a healthy shot of Pernod — similar to Louisiana's liqueur Herbsaint — to further enhance the flavors of the ingredients.

To make the stock: Clean and cut the vegetables into $1/2$-inch rounds. In a large, wide pot, heat 6 tablespoons of olive oil and brown the vegetables at a high heat, stirring frequently, until they are deeply colored, 15 to 20 minutes. Add the thyme, bay leaves, and 2 quarts of water, cover the pot, and bring to a violent boil. Add half of the crabs, cover the pot immediately, and let cook 10 minutes at a high temperature. Add the rest of the crabs and let steam another 10 minutes, until all of the crabs are red. Add 5 quarts of water and bring to a boil, skim off the foam, and simmer uncovered for 1 hour. Strain the stock through a large colander, pressing to remove every last drop, and discard crabs and vegetables. You should have about 3 quarts of stock. If you have more, reduce a little; if you're a little short, add enough water to make 3 quarts.

To make the roux: heat the olive oil very hot over a high heat and add the flour, stirring constantly with a long-handled whisk until the roux is a medium brown color. Remove from the heat and add the vegetables and the spice mix. Continue stirring for about 3 minutes, and return to the heat. Add the hot stock incrementally, stirring; allow the soup to return to a boil after each addition. Then add the tomato paste, Pernod, orange zest, and bay leaves. Simmer uncovered for about 20 minutes.

To serve, bring the soup back to a boil and cook the crawfish in it, about 5 minutes or until they are bright red. Remove and reserve the crawfish, and poach the fish for about 3 minutes. Remove and reserve the fish, and then cook the mussels in the soup, covered, just until they open, about 3 minutes. Meanwhile, divide the fish fillets into individual serving bowls, cover with the soup and the cooked mussels, and display the crawfish or langoustines on top. Garnish with 2-inch chive sticks and fried croutons.

**The Stock**

4 carrots

2 onions

2 large celery stalks, with leaves

greens of 2 leeks

(save the white parts for the soup)

olive oil

1 sprig thyme

4 bay leaves

5 pounds live small crabs

**The Roux**

1 cup olive oil

1 cup all-purpose flour

3 onions, finely chopped

1 celery stalk, finely chopped

the pulp of 5 tomatoes, peeled and chopped

1 leek (white and light green part), finely chopped

the cloves of 1 head of garlic, minced

1 large fennel bulb, cut in fine strips

**Spice Mix**

$1 1/2$ teaspoons saffron

1 tablespoon herbes de Provence

1 teaspoon ground cayenne pepper

2 teaspoons salt

2 teaspoons ground white pepper

$3/4$ cup tomato paste

1 cup Pernod

3 bay leaves

**The Fish**

16 crawfish or langoustines

8 small fillets of merlan (whiting)

8 small fillets of rouget barbet (red mullet)

8 pieces of rascasse fillet

(redfish or red snapper)

48 mussels

**Garnish**

the zest of $1/2$ orange

chive sticks and fried croutons to garnish

# Roasted Rosemary Potatoes

SERVES 8

Preheat the oven to 400°F. Wash the potatoes well, but don't peel them. While still damp, place them in one layer in a baking dish and rub them with the olive oil and the rosemary. Sprinkle with the sea salt and the crushed peppercorns. Roast, shaking the pan once or twice, for about 45 minutes until golden and crusty on the exterior and soft and creamy inside.

2 pounds tiny fingerling potatoes

3 tablespoons olive oil

handful of fresh rosemary sprigs, stems removed

sea salt

crushed black pepper

# Cajun Gazpacho

SERVES 8

**This recipe uses uncooked eggs to bind the soup. There is enough acid in the vinegar and tomato juice to kill salmonella bacteria, but if you have concerns about using raw eggs, omit them, reduce the vinegar by half, and process the vegetables a little more.**

To peel the tomatoes, drop them for 10 seconds in boiling water, then refresh them in cold water; the skin will come right off. Cut them in half and squeeze them over a sieve to catch the seeds. Mix the fresh tomato juice with the cider vinegar, olive oil, carrot purée, the quart of tomato juice, and the Louisiana Gold. Reserve.

Peel and cut the cucumber in 1-inch pieces. Remove the seeds and membranes of the pepper and cut peppers in 1-inch pieces as well. Put these vegetables aside with the tomato pulp.

Cut the onion, celery, and leek into small pieces and place in the bowl of a food processor with the garlic. Purée, adding a bit of the reserved tomato juice mixture to aid in liquifying. Add a few pieces of pepper, tomato, and cucumber, and process with the liquid. The result should be fairly smooth — no large chunks of veggies — but with body. Pour into a large bowl. Continue to blend all the vegetables with all the liquid working with the food processor. For best results, fill the bowl of the processor only half full of veggies and add the liquid through the feed tube.

When all the veggies have been blended with all the liquid, add the celery salt, white and red pepper, and corn. Reserve in the refrigerator at least 1 hour and taste. Correct the seasoning if necessary. To serve, decorate with chopped fresh cilantro and croutons, if desired.

2 pounds large ripe tomatoes

4 tablespoons cider vinegar

½ cup olive oil

about ½ cup carrot purée (optional)

1 quart tomato juice

1 tablespoon Louisiana Gold Hot Sauce

1 long or 2 short cucumbers

2 red bell peppers

1 onion

1 large celery stalk

1 leek, white and light green part

2 garlic cloves, crushed

1 teaspoon celery salt

½ teaspoon ground white pepper

a pinch or two of crushed red pepper

the kernels of 2 to 3 ears of fresh, sweet corn or 1 can of corn

fresh chopped cilantro and croutons for garnish

# Vegetarian Pannequets with Grilled Red Pepper Sauce à l'Espelette

SERVES 4; YIELDS 3 PANNEQUETS
PER PERSON

**Although this recipe is not Cajun, it is typical of our restaurant. Yves Serrano, a talented young chef from Perpignon developed it while we were racking our brains for a novel dish that evoked the Cajun spirit but contained no meat products. I've included it for two reasons: it's a French-Spanish interpretation of Louisiana cuisine, and it's a delicious vegetarian dish that you don't need to be vegetarian to appreciate. Serve it with basmati rice mixed with chopped fresh cilantro and basil leaves.**

Cut the eggplant in half lengthwise. With the cut-part down on a cutting board, slice the eggplant lengthwise in thin ⅛-inch slices. Repeat with all of the eggplants until you have 24 long slices. Plunge them in boiling water for 30 seconds, drain them, and let them rest on paper or kitchen towels to remove the excess liquid.

Cut the zucchini into 12 slices of ¼-inch width and lightly brown them on both sides on a hot raised grill pan or under the broiler. Reserve. Cut the goat cheese into twelve ½-inch rounds and reserve. Choose 12 tomates confites and 12 large basil leaves.

Form a cross with 2 slices of the blanched eggplant, the longest slice first. In the center of the cross, place the following one on top of the other: 1 zucchini slice, 1 goat cheese round, 1 tomate confite, and 1 basil leaf. Close the parcel by first bringing the 2 interior ends of the eggplant toward the center, and then the 2 exterior ends. Keep closed with a toothpick.

Preheat the oven to 375°F. Have on hand a baking dish or sheet large enough to accommodate all the pannequets. In a nonstick or cast-iron skillet, heat a little olive oil and lightly brown the bottoms of 2 or 3 pannequets at a time. Transfer to the baking dish: remove the toothpick and turn the pannequet over into the baking dish. When all the pannequets are in the baking dish, place it in the oven and bake 10 minutes.

While the pannequets bake, heat the Grilled Red Pepper Sauce (page 136) in a small saucepan or in a microwave. Serve the pannequets drizzled with or placed on a pool of sauce, accompanied by basmati rice with mixed raw herbs.

---

**For the Pannequets**

4 long eggplants, peeled

1 long or 2 small zucchini, unpeeled

10-ounce log of goat cheese, cut into 12 rounds

12 Tomates Confits (page 136), or sun-dried tomatoes soaked in hot water and drained

12 fresh basil leaves (chop the rest of the bunch for the rice)

**Liqueur table at the Laura Plantation.**

# Tomates Confits

These are better than commercial sun-dried tomatoes. Make more than you need several days in advance. They keep at least 2 weeks submerged in olive oil in the refrigerator and liven up nearly everything.

Preheat the oven to 200°F. Cut the tomatoes in 1/4-inch rounds and place them without overlapping on a baking sheet lined with plastic wrap. (Don't worry — the plastic wrap won't melt at this low temperature.) Sprinkle the tomatoes with a pinch of sugar, pepper, herbes de Provence, and a drizzle of olive oil. Bake for 4 to 6 hours, until very shrivelled but still slightly moist.

# Grilled Red Pepper Sauce with Piment de l'Espelette

This sauce can be made the night before and refrigerated. If you can't find *piment de l'Espelette*, a special ground red pepper from the Basque region, use good-quality red pepper flakes.

Preheat the oven as hot as possible. Place the red bell peppers directly on the oven rack and allow to blacken, about 20 to 30 minutes. Once nearly all black, remove from the oven with tongs and place in well-closed plastic bag or a large bowl covered with plastic wrap for about 1/2 hour. The steam from the peppers will finish the cooking and allow the skin to easily come off, once cool enough to handle. Peel off the skin and remove the seeds and stem, and with a paper towel, remove as much of the black bits as possible. Purée the peppers in a processor with the V8 or tomato juice, and add the olive oil, salt, pepper, and *piment de l'Espelette* by small pinches to taste.

2 large red bell peppers
2 tablespoons V8 or tomato juice
1 tablespoon olive oil
salt, pepper, and *piment de l'Espelette*

# Desserts

## Miss Novalene's Sweet Potato Pie

**This recipe comes from Houston, Texas, from our friend Mo Roberts's great-great-aunt Miss Novalene.**

Preheat the oven to 350°F. Roll out the dough and fit it in a 9-inch pie pan. Remove the pulp from the yams and whisk it with all the other ingredients until smooth. Pour the filling into the pie pan and crimp the edges of the dough. Bake 45 minutes. Serve warm or room temperature, with whipped cream if desired.

1 recipe Pâte Sucrée (below)

2 yams or orange sweet potatoes (about 2 pounds), baked 1 hour in a 400°F oven

3 eggs, lightly beaten

1 cup light brown sugar

¼ cup whole milk

1 teaspoon baking powder

1 tablespoon all-purpose flour

1 teaspoon vanilla extract

½ teaspoon ground cinnamon

½ teaspoon ground nutmeg

## PIE CRUSTS

# Pâte Sucrée (Sweet Crust)

YIELDS 1 NINE-INCH CRUST

Mix the flour, confectioner's sugar, and salt in a mixer with a dough paddle. Add the butter and blend until the mixture resembles dry oatmeal. Add the egg and mix just until the dough begins to hold together. Don't overwork. Knead with your hands for 5 seconds, form a ball, and flatten, forming a ³/₄-inch-thick disk. Cover with plastic wrap and refrigerate at least 2 hours or overnight. To roll out, place the disk of dough on a lightly floured surface, sprinkle with a little flour, and roll out to ¹/₈-inch thickness.

1 ¹/₃ cups all-purpose flour

1 tablespoon confectioners' sugar

1 pinch of salt

8 tablespoons very cold unsalted butter (1 stick), cut in small pieces

1 egg

# Pâte Brisée (Short Crust)

YIELDS 2 NINE-INCH CRUSTS

Put the flour and salt in the bowl of a mixer with a dough paddle, and incorporate the butter quickly, until it resembles dry oatmeal. Add the egg and 2 tablespoons of cold water, and rapidly mix just until the dough begins to hold together. If it seems to dry or crumbly, incorporate the other 2 tablespoons of water, being careful not to over-mix. Form 2 balls, cover each with a piece of plastic wrap and flatten into ³/₄-inch-thick disks. Refrigerate at least 2 hours or overnight. To roll out, place the disk of dough on a lightly floured surface, sprinkle with a little flour, and roll out to ¹/₈-inch thickness.

2 cups all-purpose flour

1 teaspoon salt

12 tablespoons very cold unsalted butter (1 ½ sticks), cut in small cubes

1 egg

2 to 4 tablespoons very cold water

# Apple Pie

**This is the ultra-traditional American Apple Pie, delicious in its simplicity. You will need a 9- to 10-inch deep dish pie pan, and a pastry brush.**

6 to 8 Granny Smith or other firm, tart apples

1 recipe Pâte Brisée (page 139)

4 to 6 tablespoons light brown sugar

juice of one lemon

2 tablespoons all-purpose flour

$\frac{1}{2}$ teaspoon grated nutmeg

1 teaspoon cinnamon

1 egg, beaten with 1 tablespoon water

A few hours or the night before baking, peel, core, and cut the apples into $\frac{3}{4}$-inch slices and sprinkle them with the lemon juice, sugar, nutmeg, and cinnamon. Allow the flavors to meld in a tightly covered container in the refrigerator for several hours.

Preheat the oven to 400°F. Roll out half of the dough and fit it into a buttered and floured pie pan, leaving a 1-inch overhang. Brush the bottom and sides of the dough with half of the egg mixture. This will prevent the apple juices from soaking the bottom crust. Sprinkle the apple mixture with the flour and mound it into the pie tin so that the center is higher than the rest. Roll out the second half of the dough and fit it on top of the apples. Cut off the excess; it should be about $\frac{1}{2}$ inch smaller than the bottom. Fold the overhang from the bottom crust over the edge of the top crust and pinch to seal. With a knife, cut four small symmetrical slits on the top of the pie to allow steam to escape. Paint the top of the pie with the egg glaze.

Bake the pie for 10 to 12 minutes 400°F. Turn the oven down to 350°F and cook 40 to 45 minutes longer, until the dough is golden and the apples tender.

Allow to cool to lukewarm before cutting. Serve with vanilla ice cream or crème fraîche, if desired.

# Mississippi Mud Pie

**The Crust**

9 ounces chocolate cookies (about 10 cookies)

6 tablespoons unsalted butter, melted

$\frac{1}{2}$ teaspoon salt

**The Mud**

8 tablespoons unsalted butter (1 stick)

4 ounces semisweet chocolate, chopped

1 teaspoon vanilla extract

4 tablespoons very strong espresso

3 tablespoons dark Karo syrup (preferred) or honey

2 tablespoons heavy cream

3 eggs, very cold

$1\frac{1}{3}$ cups sugar

6 ounces roasted salted peanuts, chopped

Reduce the cookies to fine crumbs in a food processor. In a bowl, mix them with the melted butter and salt. Butter the bottom and sides of a 10-inch springform pan and press the crumbs on the bottom and partway up the sides. Refrigerate. Remove the pan from the refrigerator just before filling.

Melt the butter and the chocolate together in a saucepan or in a microwave. Allow to cool to lukewarm. Stir in the vanilla. Preheat the oven to 350°F. In a small bowl, mix the espresso, Karo syrup, and the cream and set aside.

Beat the cold eggs in a mixer (recommended) or with a whisk, until light in color.

Little by little, add the sugar while beating. When the mixture is very thick, alternately add the chocolate mixture and the coffee mixture while beating. When the consistency is that of a mousse, stir in about two-thirds of the chopped peanuts.

Scrape the mixture into the springform pan and sprinkle with the remaining peanuts. Bake 50 minutes. The pie will rise when cooked and fall and crack while cooling. Once cool, refrigerate in its mold. Once cold, run a knife soaked in hot water around the circumference of the pie before removing the outside ring. Allow to return to room temperature before serving.

# Louisiana Bread Pudding with Bourbon Sauce

**SERVES 12**

Soak the bread in the milk for 1 hour in a large bowl. Butter an 8 x 11-inch pan. When the bread is saturated, preheat the oven to 300°F.

Beat the eggs, sugar, and vanilla with a whisk. Pour the mixture into the bowl with the milk-soaked bread. Add the rasins and mix well with a spoon. Pour everything into the buttered pan and smooth it with the back of a spoon. Sprinkle with the cinnamon, nutmeg, and dark brown sugar, then with the butter cubes. Bake about 1 $\frac{1}{2}$ hours; when it's set, it's cooked. Allow to cool 30 minutes before cutting. Serve with Bourbon Sauce (see below), or with maple syrup for kids. Bread Pudding reheats beautifully in the oven or in a microwave.

7 ounces (about 1 baguette) very stale French bread, cut into cubes
1 quart whole milk
3 eggs
1 $\frac{1}{3}$ cups sugar
2 tablespoons vanilla extract
$\frac{1}{2}$ cup raisins soaked in Cointreau or kirsch
1 tablespoon cinnamon
1 teaspoon ground nutmeg
$\frac{1}{2}$ cup packed dark brown sugar
12 tablespoons unsalted butter (1 $\frac{1}{2}$ sticks), cut into small cubes

## BOURBON SAUCE

Melt the butter in a saucepan over low heat. When hot but not colored, add the confectioner's sugar while beating with a whisk. Once it's very thick and hot, remove from the heat and whisk in the beaten egg; beat until emulsified, a couple of minutes. Whisk in the bourbon. Serve warm.

8 tablespoons unsalted butter (1 stick)
$\frac{1}{2}$ cup confectioners' sugar
1 egg, beaten
$\frac{1}{2}$ cup bourbon

# Carrot Cake with Cream Cheese Icing

**SERVES 12**

Preheat the oven to 350°F. Butter and flour a 9 x 4 x 2-inch loaf cake pan. Mix the flour, salt, baking powder, and cinnamon, and set aside. With a whisk or in a mixer, beat the oil, sugar, vanilla, carrot purée, and the eggs until smooth. Stir in the flour mixture, and then the pecans and chopped carrot. Scrape into the loaf pan and bake 1 $\frac{1}{2}$ hours, or until a knife inserted in the center comes out clean. Cool completely before unmolding and icing.

To make the icing, mix the confectioner's sugar, cinnamon, and salt; set aside. Beat the butter, cream cheese, and vanilla with a whisk or in a mixer (much easier!) until light and fluffy. Slowly add the sugar mixture while continuing to beat.

To ice the carrot cake, apply the icing in swirls with a spatula. Cover the iced cake with plastic wrap and refrigerate a few hours for easier slicing. Cut while cold and leave at room temperature 15 to 30 minutes before serving.

1 $\frac{1}{3}$ cups all-purpose flour
$\frac{1}{2}$ teaspoon salt
$\frac{1}{2}$ tablespoon baking powder
2 $\frac{1}{2}$ teaspoons cinnamon
$\frac{3}{4}$ cup sunflower seed oil
2 $\frac{1}{3}$ cups sugar
$\frac{1}{2}$ tablespoon vanilla extract
$\frac{1}{4}$ cup cooked carrots, puréed
2 eggs
4 ounces pecans, chopped
1 large raw carrot, finely chopped in a food processor

**Cream Cheese Icing**

1 pound 10 ounces confectioners' sugar
1 tablespoon cinnamon
$\frac{1}{2}$ teaspoon salt
8 tablespoons unsalted butter (1 stick), at room temperature
8 ounces cream cheese, at room temperature
1 tablespoon vanilla extract

# Brownies

YIELDS 12 BROWNIES

Line an 8 x 11 x 1-inch pan with parchment paper, or butter the pan. Preheat the oven to 325°F.

Cut the chocolate and butter in small pieces and melt together, either in the microwave or in a saucepan over very low heat. Mix well and allow to return to room temperature. Add the vanilla.

Lightly beat the eggs with a whisk or in a mixer, and add the sugar while beating. Stir in the chocolate/butter mixture with a large spoon. Stir in the flour, just until mixed, and one half of the pecans. Do not overmix. Spread the batter evenly in the pan, sprinkle with the remaining pecans and bake 20 to 23 minutes, just until a knife inserted in the center comes out clean. Allow to cool completely before cutting.

6 ounces unsweetened or bittersweet chocolate
8 tablespoons unsalted butter (1 stick)
1 tablespoon vanilla extract
3 eggs
1 $\frac{1}{2}$ cups sugar
$\frac{2}{3}$ cup all-purpose flour
$\frac{1}{4}$ pound pecans, chopped

# Chocolate Chip Cookies

YIELDS ABOUT 2 DOZEN 2-INCH COOKIES

**This cookie recipe is the first American recipe I developed using French ingredients, which is why it calls for baking powder instead of soda, and cassonade instead of dark brown sugar. Light and buttery, these cookies stand up to comparisons.**

In a large bowl or a mixer, cream the butter and sugar. Add the egg and vanilla.

In another bowl, mix the flour, baking powder and salt, and add this mixture to the butter/sugar mixture; don't overwork. When the flour is nearly completely incorporated, add the chocolate chips and mix until they are well distributed. Allow the dough to rest at least one hour or overnight, covered with plastic wrap, in the refrigerator.

Preheat the oven to 350°F. With a small ice cream scoop or with your hands, make 1-inch balls of dough and place them 1 inch apart on an unbuttered cookie sheet. Bake 15 minutes. Allow to cool 10 to 15 minutes before removing the cookies with a spatula.

1 cup (2 sticks) unsalted butter, room temperature
1 $\frac{1}{2}$ cups light brown sugar
1 egg
1 tablespoon vanilla extract
2 cups + 2 tablespoons all-purpose flour
$\frac{1}{2}$ tablespoon baking powder
1 teaspoon salt
9 ounces chocolate chips

**Right: Room at the Oak Alley Plantation in Vacherie.**

# Lagniappe

In the eighteenth century, when Louisiana housewives went to market to buy their rice, the merchant would throw in a couple of extra handfuls after the transaction was completed to compensate for the weight of the linen sack. "Pour la nappe" (for the cloth), he would say. Over the years this developed into "lagniappe," which has come to mean "a little extra" and applies to all sorts of situations, including the breads, dishes, and sauces featured here.

## Corn Bread

SERVES 12

**If you have leftover corn bread (which is rare) dry it out completely and keep it several months in an airtight container. The dried crumbs serve as a base for Thanksgiving Herbed Corn Bread Stuffing (page 67) and are an essential ingredient in the Crab Stuffing (page 86).**

Preheat the oven to 425°F. Mix all of the dry ingredients in a small bowl. In a large bowl, beat the eggs lightly with a whisk and add the milk. Melt the butter, and pour it into an 8 x 11-inch baking pan (preferably cast iron or metal), pivoting the pan to coat the bottom and sides with the melted butter. Pour the excess butter into the egg mixture and mix well. Pour the dry ingredients into the liquid ingredients and mix with a large spoon, just to moisten. Don't overmix; the batter should not be smooth and a few small lumps are desirable.

Pour the batter into the buttered pan and bake 10 to 12 minutes, until the bread is golden brown. Delicious warm (it reheats well), serve it as an accompaniment to Barbecue Ribs or Southern Fried Chicken (page 109), or with butter, honey, or jam for breakfast.

1 cup yellow corn meal

1 cup all-purpose flour

4 tablespoons sugar

1 $\frac{1}{2}$ tablespoons baking powder

1 teaspoon salt

1 tablespoon herbes de Provence

$\frac{1}{2}$ teaspoon ground sage (optional)

1 cup milk

2 whole eggs

3 $\frac{1}{2}$ tablespoons melted butter

## Buttermilk Biscuits

YIELDS 24 SMALL BISCUITS

Preheat the oven to 400°F. Mix the first five ingredients in a flat-bottomed metal bowl. Add the cold butter, two-thirds of the cheddar (reserve the rest of the cheddar for later), and 1 tablespoon of the herbes de Provence, and cut with a pastry blender or mash with a fork until the mixture resembles dry oatmeal. Make a well in the center and add the buttermilk. Stir rapidly with a large spoon just until the dough begins to hold together, then knead with your fingertips for 10 to 15 seconds, and form a large, lumpy ball. Overmixing is the death of biscuits — the uglier your dough, the lighter your biscuits.

With your fingers, pull off a walnut-sized piece of dough, quickly form a ball, and dip it first in the melted butter and then in the reserved grated cheddar. Place these balls, cheddar side up, on an unbuttered baking sheet 1 inch apart and sprinkle with a bit of herbes de Provence. Bake 10 minutes. Let cool 5 minutes before removing from the baking sheet.

2 cups all-purpose flour

1 teaspoon salt

2 teaspoons baking powder

$\frac{1}{2}$ teaspoon baking soda

1 teaspoon sugar

6 tablespoons very cold butter, cut into small cubes

2 ounces cheddar cheese, grated

herbes de Provence

1 cup buttermilk

$\frac{1}{2}$ cup butter, melted

**Preceding spread, left: Interior of Acadian Village in Lafayette.
Preceding spread, right: Stalls at the Farmer's Market in New Orleans.**

# Fried Seafood

Along with fried shrimp and crawfish tails, fried oysters and scallops are adored all over South. Difficult to make in large quantities, they are best reserved for a few close friends. This recipe, which doesn't use an egg–milk dip to adhere the flour mix to the seafood, results in a light, crispy coating.

---

⅓ cup corn flour

⅓ cup all-purpose flour

1 tablespoon Spice Mix for Cooking (page 20)

vegetable oil for frying

12 medium shrimp or crawfish tails, 12 large oysters, or 12 scallops (or a mix)

1 recipe Table Spice Mix (page 20)

Heat the oil to 375°F in a large skillet at about 1-inch depth. In a bag, place the seafood (one species at a time) with the first three ingredients and shake to coat. Toss them immediately into the hot oil and fry just until they are golden. Drain on paper towels and sprinkle with Table Spice Mix. Enjoy immediately!

## COCKTAIL SAUCE

YIELDS ABOUT 1 CUP

**Serve as an accompaniment to cold boiled shrimp or crawfish tails.**

---

1 cup ketchup

scant 2 tablespoons prepared horseradish sauce

1 tablespoon fresh lemon juice

1 tablespoon Louisiana hot sauce

1 teaspoon Worcestershire sauce

2 pinches each of celery salt, ground cayenne pepper, ground mustard, allspice

Mix all ingredients together with a whisk and serve very cold.

## SAUCE MARIGNY

YIELDS ABOUT 1 CUP

**This sweet/spicy sauce is perfect for fried shrimp and crawfish tails, or fried scallops and vegetable tempuras.**

---

½ twelve-ounce jar bitter orange marmalade

½ twelve-ounce jar apricot preserves

5 tablespoons prepared horseradish

5 tablespoons Dijon mustard

3 tablespoons Louisiana hot sauce

1 tablespoon ginger vinegar (or 1 tablespoon fresh chopped ginger infused for one hour in 4 tablespoons rice vinegar, then strained)

Whisk all together until smooth.

## TARTAR SAUCE

The basis for this recipe was given to me by one of the owners of a well-known Southern chain of fried-food restaurants; we added the tarragon and celery salt.

---

1 cup Basic Mayonnaise (page 115)

½ cup dill pickles, finely chopped, with a little juice

2 tablespoons chopped capers

2 teaspoons fresh lemon juice

a few drops Louisiana hot sauce

½ teaspoon freshly ground black pepper

1 teaspoon finely chopped fresh parsley

2 teaspoons crumbled dried tarragon

1 pinch of celery salt, or to taste

Mix everything together and chill. Everything should be chopped by hand; the finer the ingredients are chopped, the better the sauce.

Serve with Fried Seafood (left) or Louisiana Crab Cakes (page 97).

**This page: A table at Mulate's restaurant in Breaux Bridge.**
**Page 154: Bedroom at Laura Plantation.**

# Recipe Index

# Useful Addresses

**Thanksgiving Restaurant**
20, rue Saint-Paul
75004 Paris
tel. 33 1 42 77 68 28
Judith and Frédéric Bluysen's restaurant.

**Thanksgiving Grocery**
14, rue Charles V
75004 Paris
tel. 33 1 42 77 68 29
American grocery products and kitchen utensils, catering service.

## WHERE TO STAY AND DINE IN LOUISIANA

### IN NEW ORLEANS

**Antoine's Restaurant**
713–717 rue Saint Louis
New Orleans, LA 70130
tel. (504) 581-4422
Family-owned restaurant established in 1840, serving French/Creole cuisine.

**Galatoire's Restaurant**
209 Bourbon Street
New Orleans, LA 70130
tel. (504) 525-2021
Legendary New Orleans Creole cuisine in the heart of the French Quarter.

**Hôtel Le Cirque**
2 Lee Circle
New Orleans, LA 70130
tel. (504) 962-0900
Very modern design.

**Hôtel Maison Orléans**
904 Iberville Street
New Orleans, LA 70112
tel. (703) 534-8100
Luxurious.

**K-Paul's Louisiana Kitchen**
416 Chartres Street
New Orleans, LA 70130
tel. (504) 524-7394
Owned by celebrity chef Paul Prudhomme.

**Soniat House Hotel**
1133 Chartres Street
New Orleans, LA 70116
tel. (504) 522-0570
Magnificent French Quarter mansion furnished with French antiques.

## AROUND LAFAYETTE, THE CENTER OF CAJUN CULTURE

**Bois des chênes**
Bed and Breakfast
338 N. Sterling Street
(corner of Mudd Avenue)
Lafayette, Louisiana 70501
tel. (337) 233-7816
Friendly and comfortable. The owner, Coerte Voorhies, organizes tours of the Atchafalaya River.

**Bayou Cabins**
100 Mills Avenue
Breaux Bridge, LA 70517
tel. (318) 332-6158
Authentic Cajun cabins. Rustic but very comfortable.

**D.I.'s Restaurant**
6533 Evangeline Hwy
Basile, LA 70515
tel. (337) 432-5141
Family-style Cajun cuisine, music, and dance.

**Mulate's Restaurant**
325 Mills Avenue
Breaux Bridge, LA 70617
tel. (337) 332-4648
Lively bar and restaurant, with Cajun music and dance.

## PLANTATIONS WITH ACCOMMODATIONS

**Oak Alley Plantation**
3645 Louisiana Highway 18
Vacherie, LA 70090
tel. (800) 463-7138
Built in 1839, one of the South's oldest plantations.

**Nottoway Plantation**
30970 Highway 405 (River Road)
White Castle, LA 70788
tel. (225) 545-2730
Dating from 1859, this elegant plantation exemplifies life in the "Old South."

**Chretien Point Plantation**
665 Chretien Point Road
Sunset, LA 70584
tel. (800) 880-7050
Smaller than the two preceding plantations, but more intimate and just as lovely.

**Laura Plantation**
2247 Louisiana Highway 18
Vacherie, LA 70090
tel. (888) 265-7960
The Creole universe is depicted in this beautifully preserved and furnished 1805 structure. Bed-and-breakfast opening end of 2003.

**Louisiana Office of Tourism**
PO Box 94291
Baton Rouge, LA 70804-9291
tel. (800) 677-4082

## ACKNOWLEDGMENTS

Judith Bluysen and Jean-Marie and Esin del Moral wish to thank Staub Cookware France, the Soulant family, and Bruce Foods Corporation, New Iberia, LA; and Simon Rathle, Quim Gener, Scott Breaux, Fran Thobodeaux, Coerte Voorhies, Christine De Cuir, Jeff Richards, Kelly Strenge, Debra Credeur, and Charlotte Hamel, for their help with the photographs taken in Louisiana.

For help with the food styling, they also wish to thank the following:

**Jeanine Cros**
11, rue d'Assas 75006 Paris
tel. 01 45 48 00 67
for loaning napkins, dishcloths, and tablecloths

**Régine Painvin, Boutique Flamand**
8, rue de Fürstenberg, 75006 Paris
tel. 01 56 81 12 40
for loaning dishes and tableware

**Boutique Potiron**
57, rue des Petits-Champs, 75001 Paris
tel. 01 40 15 00 38
for loaning dishes and bowls

**Boutique Mis en Demeure**
27, rue du Cherche-Midi, 75006 Paris
tel. 01 45 48 83 79
for loaning dishes and glassware

**Boutique Thym Thé d'Ailleurs**
22, rue Saint-Paul, 75004 Paris
for loaning trays and dishes